We Will Remember

Remember

The Life of Bill and Lily McEvoy

Kieran McEvoy

✤

This book is dedicated to my sister Marian,
the gem of our family.

Acknowledgments

I especially thank Debbie McClain for her encouragement while writing this book and all of her helpful editing skills. God provided you to me, Debbie, to keep me on track and fulfill my father's commission.

We Will Remember

As a young boy, barely three, my older brother and I would love to play bronco by jumping on my mother's back and riding her like a wild horse. One day after playing for a while, my mother sat up on the floor and said, "I wonder when you grow up someday, will you remember me playing with you like this?" Both my brother and I wrapped our arms around her neck, exclaiming, "Mom, we will never forget you playing with us; we will always remember."

The story of my parents, two remarkable people from Ireland will inspire all who read this accurate account of their lives. They were each born in the poverty of an Ireland that had just become a sovereign, free nation. Their lives would rise from obscurity and touch the lives of people everywhere throughout Ireland, the United States and Canada.

Contents

"Thus we never see the true state of our condition till it is illustrated to us by its contraries, nor how to value what we enjoy but by the want of it."

—Daniel Defoe, Robinson Crusoe

Preface

The story of my parents left an indelible impact on my life and the lives of so many others. With both of them now gone, there is hardly a day that does not bring reflection on two lives sorely missed. I miss the many days and years of stopping in to visit with my mother, or sitting with my father hearing his evocative stories of life and love of his native country Ireland.

After my father's death, my son sent me a text one day in response to a picture I had sent him of my father. "Love this, Dad. I miss Pop Pop a lot, more than I thought I would have." A while ago, I passed through a section of woods in Islip, where overnight, a massive tree had fallen, puncturing a gaping hole in the green canopy. I never noticed the tree before, but then, I profoundly sensed its absence, the way its arms had upheld the lofty mantle above, and shielded the forest floor below from the sun's intense heat. It lay there on the forest floor, the smell of fresh earth in overturned roots permeating the scene, its glorious trunk strange and unfittingly on its side. Pop Pop was a massive oak, his span was, for me, only fully comprehended by the void he left behind. Multiple saplings would doubtless grow to fill the void, though none would replace the form.

It is for those saplings of my parents this book is written and dedicated, that they might also one day as lofty mantles glorify God in His calling upon each of their lives.

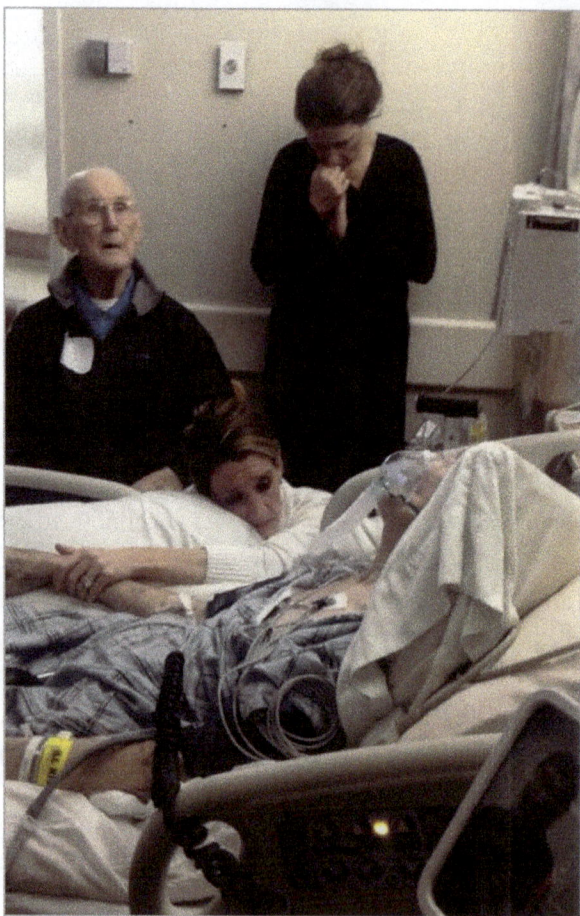

Introduction

I have reflected several times since my mother's death on October 21, 2016 that only once do I remember Mom not able to rise, put on the kettle, and place a favorite meal before me. It was in those couple of days before she died as she lay on her hospital bed with all of her children around her and my father sitting at her side. Her inability to get up was a thought incongruous to who she was and had always been, as she lay there conscious but quiet and still. A scarf over my mother's head revealed her dignity and beauty that even when dying she was not to be seen by her family with the thinning hair of old age.

A life was now coming to an end that was larger than any other life I had ever known. She would look straight up when I came into the hospital room to call me by my pet name Keeney, that she would so often say with endearment. We knew her long battle with Parkinson's disease was coming to an end, but this disease that would end her life was less hurtful to her than the loss of my sister Marian who had died only several months before.

The loss of Marian had substantially reduced my mother's will to live which she often communicated to me when I was alone with her. Marian was the gem of our family, and the most caring of all siblings towards my parents. There was not ever a day that Marian missed calling my parents or visiting them at their home. It had been the most crushing blow to the lives of both of my parents, and had completely taken away from my mother the will to live.

On that final night of communication with my mother I had brought with me at my son's suggestion, pictures in an album, that he had provided of his twin daughters that were born only months before. My mother had not seen her great granddaughters who were born and lived in Arizona with my son and his wife and our lovely grandson Connor.

As I placed the album before my mother's eyes I said "Hey Mom, here are Mara and Avery. You will never see them, but you will live through them as they grow. They are your great granddaughters that you have never held. Aren't they beautiful?"

As I turned each page my mother's face lit up and changed as if it had been the face of an angel. It had been such a good suggestion by my son Sean because it touched that area of my mother from where all her circuits were wired, and that part of her life where electricity continually flowed.

She loved her children, all of her children. When grandchildren came, it was as if it started all over again. She had a connection to each of their lives with a love that was insurmountable and understood by each one of them in a way that was very personal.

Less than two days before, Mom had been walking around the hospital floor with my wife and sisters. Now a dispensation was coming to an end and it was apparent to all of us, including my father. How could our lives go on and be the same without Mom?

It presented an equation to each of us that no one could answer. The pathos of that night and following day would seem reminiscent of a picture from the "Last Supper" where sorrow filled everyone's heart, and many tears flowed at the impending departure of someone dearly loved.

My mom had finished her course. She raised nine children singlehandedly with indomitable energy while my father worked two full time jobs. Her twenty-five grandchildren were just as much a part of her life as her own children, and at the time of her death it was certainly clear that her great grandchildren would exceed the number of grandchildren.

As a young boy, I had looked upon my father as someone who could surmount any problem or difficulty. As the patriarch of our family, he was now sitting beside his wife of sixty-five years, losing the person he had so dearly loved. Our sister Marian's death months earlier had already devastated him. My father now sat in quiet dignity and composure, comforted by his children, especially his daughters who had such capacity to love him with the deepest affection. Everyone's sorrow was beyond words. Our mother was the most integral part of our family and our lives were inextricably connected to her.

Over six years now have passed since my mother's departure. My father is also gone for over two years now from the time of this writing. It was the wish of my father before his death that my mother's story be written. I was able to spend many evenings with him and gather information and stories that I did not know about. It was my greatest wish that this book be written and finished for my father to have read. It was not to be. It was during the time six months before my father's death that I became sick with a very inexplicable sleep disorder that rapidly changed my world in just a matter of weeks. Although I visited my father each day as always, the writing stopped. I had been making such progress up to that point and relished each day of my father's input on my mother's history, and her unfolding story.

In a series of confluencing events with health, my wife and I had decided to sell our homes in New York and Arizona and move to Tennessee where our oldest son lived. Just a week before we were to move, my father died after being sick for only a few days. Perhaps this has been the most painful period of my life to lose my father who was my best friend and partner in business, and to leave the beautiful home where I raised my children. Nearly every month we would travel out to our second home which I still sorely miss.

But it has since stayed on my heart to finish my father's commission, and now a year and eight months later I have decided to continue writing this book as a narrative of my mother and father's journey. I believe they have a unique and interesting story, and a story that should be told; the story of the lives of Elisabeth and Bill McEvoy.

I have no expectation of this book being read by anyone except for those connected to their lives as friends, and those within our family tree. Perhaps years from now, when siblings, grandchildren and great grand-children are no longer remembered, the progeny of future generations might be inspired to take courage and have faith in God, to overcome the great trials of life and enter the promised land granted to those who have faith and never give up, even in the face of daunting challenges.

If this book is to have any value at all it must be accurate and not embellished, nor should any attempt be made to accomplish an attractive literary style. I would find this to be detracting from the lives of two truly great people who already have a great story that does not require any embellishment.

So may the lambs of our fold and the future whelps of our clan hear the story of their great progenitors Elisabeth and William McEvoy who left Ireland and poverty to begin a new life here in the United States.

At the time of this writing eight of their nine children are still alive. Twenty-five grandchildren and thirty-five great grandchildren survive my parents, as what would appear an exponential equation, testifying of two lives that met and the faithfulness of God and the fulfilling of His covenant upon their lives.

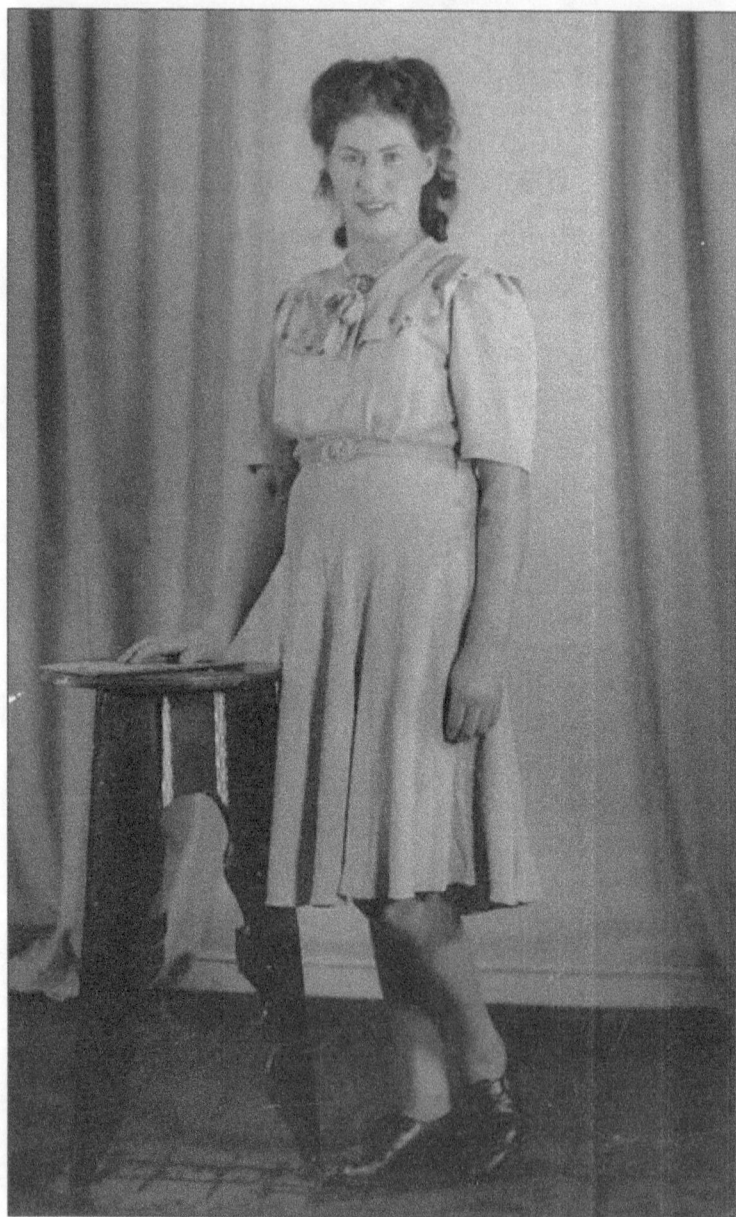

Mom as a young woman

Chapter 1

Mother Grows Up in Banemore, Ireland

It was during the time defined as a "global pandemic" of Covid 19 that my father commissioned me to write my mother's story. During that April of 2020 my mom had already been gone three and a half years. The world seemed reeling as millions of people were dying from this epidemic, and entire economies were shut down. As my father was 97 years young at that time, he had remained very lucid and contemplative. He missed my mother terribly. He shared regrets about time spent away from her as he traveled throughout North America building chapters for Irish music and making around 138 trips back to Ireland.

It was during that time when I would regularly visit each day that I asked my father his thoughts on such an enterprise as writing my mom's story. In my father's very words, he said, "Kieran, if you are going to write a book on your mother's life, it must be written from your own perspective, but please take the time to be disciplined, that it be accomplished." My father spoke to me from the sentiments of his own life, he got things done. I saw him do this over the course of many decades in business, and perhaps I was that way in business too. It would be a far more difficult challenge and undertaking for me to write a book. My father was a naturally gifted at all these tasks. He was always writing and on the phone, setting up Irish cultural and music events, talking to and staying connected to his Irish friends. He was a very self-motivated man.

To honor my parents and their story will entail that a new discipline and commitment be engaged and the copious process of writing and gathering information be commenced. To endeavor to see our children and grandchildren and those who follow after receive inspiration from two such commendable lives. And in doing so, many descendants might courageously accept the baton passed to them by their notable ancestors. That all the progeny of Elizabeth and Bill McEvoy may run their race with the same strength and fortitude.

It is therefore a joy for me to begin this book by sharing my mother's story first. I know this would be my father's desire. My father had no thought when this project was started that his life story was also to be included. In only a matter of months from the time I began writing, the great patriarch of our family was to be with his bride and sorely missed love, our mother.

So here is the story of my mother that begins with her as a young girl in Ireland, her native country. The stories are ones that I heard directly from my mother, and in conversations with my father and other related people. My mother was a great story teller. As young children we would be mesmerized by her accounts of adventure and hardship that she experienced while growing up. Her best stories were told by defining moments in her life where there would be intersections with destiny. Intersections that would affect you the reader and also become part of your story. It is sobering that many of the decisions made in life have a ripple effect that can influence the life of future generations. How important that my mother though not a perfect person was a woman of faith and surrendered to God. Her life was a tapestry that on one side did not look beautiful or promising, but on the other side a picture of a beautiful life unfolded that was blessed by God as one stamped for favor and mercy.

Elizabeth Kelliher was born January 15, 1924 in County Kerry, in an obscure elevated area outside the quaint town of Listowel called Banemore. My mother would be called Lily her whole life by family and close friends. The natural splendor of County Kerry from Banemore hill could compare favorably with any other attractive view of Ireland. Stepping away from the house which is still there today in ruins, and walking only 50 feet is a panorama of beauty and vista stretching out to the blue Atlantic Ocean in the west on the far horizon. Looking out to the far northwest, the Shannon River can be seen meandering in the distance flowing through a kaleidoscope of emerald fields and small farms. Directly below in the distance is the world-famous golf course Ballybunyon. A large hill connecting to my mother's home called "Stacks Glen" could be a short cut from the road below if you were young and healthy and able to climb as my mother did on the way home from school each day. If one can imagine what Kerry is like, to our curious descendants, it is a county that today's tourist to Ireland never misses. It is a peninsular county with a striking terrain of mountains and rugged areas that extend out into the Atlantic Ocean. Scenic bays surround these many peninsulas creating one of the most attractive geographies of Ireland. For this reason, Kerry is considered one of Ireland's most favored tourist counties to visit. It also has the most stunning lakes that can be found anywhere in the country. My wife and I in our visits to Ireland have stayed at hotels situated in Killarney with incredible views of shimmering water, pristine landscapes and golf courses surrounded by scenic mountains.

Only a couple of years before my mother was born, the Anglo-Irish Treaty that ended the War of Independence was signed on December 6, 1922. Ireland had become a sovereign country known as the Irish Free State and had finally gained its independence from England. My father's father fought during this War of Independence and was captured and incarcerated by the British and sent to a prison in England. Because of centuries of English oppression, Ireland was impoverished when it finally became an autonomous country. A far superior country militarily had kept Ireland as a vassal state to supply its needs with agriculture and beef and other items as its empire stretched across the globe. Throughout much of its history Irish farmers were like feudal tenants working for English landowners.

In my mother's childhood nearly everyone was poor and poverty was universally understood, but not accepted by my mother. It would take many years before Ireland would become the economically stable country that it is today. My mother's life and happiness were never defined by money, but her vision was to raise a family where her children would not be forced to leave and emigrate to a part of the world where she would never see them again.

My mother was born the youngest of eleven children in the very home where both I and my older brother Patrick were born, my mother's parents being considerably older meant that as a young girl she would not see some of her older siblings who had already emigrated to America. From a very early age my mother would learn the responsibilities of life on a farm. She would learn to make butter and bread, milk cows, and butcher chickens, and cook meals.

As a young girl my mother walked several miles to school each day. By cutting across Stacks Glen, she saved some distance but it would require navigating a steep vale. Each day before school several chores needed to be accomplished, and then a long trek undertaken to get to school on time. After school there would be another long walk back and upon arriving home additional chores were performed.

As a young girl her mother's health began to fail. More and more my mother found herself becoming involved with the domestic duties of the home. Eventually her mother would become bed stricken with paralysis and my mother's education would not continue.

It is often thought that each of us is born with a temperament that pretty much stays with us throughout life. My mother from the earliest age had an indomitable spirit that was incapable of passivity and surrender, despite what might appear to be insurmountable. It would only be later in life after the death of my sister, Marian that I would see my mother sit in quiet melancholy. Yet within that time of sorrow, my mother would still connect with her other children, grandchildren and great grandchildren and draw strength from the intimacy and affection she would receive from each one of them.

My mother would tell us stories of her adventures growing up as a young girl. While today much of the fun children experience involves money and technology, my mother's Ireland provided open fields, friendly neighbors, dancehalls and music events. There were stories of the field that she was compelled to cross and the wild bull she would cleverly avoid as she endeavored to take shortcuts on the way home from surrounding areas. She would ride horses and one that was so ungovernable he would ride off at full gallop with her holding on for dear life.

There was a mischievous boy who my mother with superior strength would beat up on the way home from school. There was one occasion when several bullies waiting for my mother with aforementioned Paddy O'Brien were neutralized by my mother using her bookbag full of books as a wrecking ball. Her stories and feats of strength were very believable because growing up, my mother was the strongest woman I ever knew. As a teenager who regularly lifted weights, neither I nor any of my strongest friends could hold our hands in position without my mother pulling them apart like loose spaghetti.

My mother's gregarious nature would charm her entire class as a young girl. When the teacher on a particular day stepped out, my mother would stand in front of the map of Europe with the long pointer and recite comical quips such as "long legged Italy kicked poor Sicily into the pot of the Mediterranean Sea." The class would be laughing at her clever and witty comments, while in walked the school master with ensuing punishment. Her spontaneity and impetuous behavior would often invoke corporal chastisement that in those days was fairly routine. Any affected child would not tell their parents in order to avoid additional punishment.

My mother being denied a complete education was driven by a healthy sense of pride to never appear uneducated. All nine of her mostly college educated children would not possess her ability in penmanship and coherency in thought and communication. As a young girl she could never have realized that one day she would entertain future Irish senators along with renowned musicians, dignitaries and cultural leaders from Ireland in her beautiful New York home. When they would visit through my father's involvement with Irish culture and music, my mother was masterful in conversation and etiquette, always making people feel welcome and accepted. Her sense of propriety in entertaining would never diminish her ability to be forthright and sincere about subjects she held in conviction. I often wondered how my mother possessed such attributes and inner strength. She lived an insular life on a farm while also caring for a sick mother who never once told her growing up "I love you." Yet as a young girl she held the dream of emigrating to a faraway place called America. One day her poverty would be left and her children raised in a place where they could prosper and raise their families. Her dreams were defined at the earliest age as being intransigent to the thoughts and opinions of others who thought contrary and were challenged by her ideals.

She loved her children before they were ever born and would raise them in a world where they would be protected from the hardship and poverty that she had experienced. The Ireland my mother knew from a young girl reflected a country of massive emigration to other parts of the world especially the United States. This included nearly half of her own family.

My mother's mother had been born into a family far different from her own experience growing up in Banemore. My grandmother grew up in a family that would have been considered wealthy by all standards at that time. Having a large farm, they had a lot of hired men and servants. My grandmother happened to fall in love with one of them, and married far below the economic strata she had enjoyed as a young girl. My mother would share with me how her mother's parents were not happy about that relationship and recommended against it. Love had prevailed as is often the case. In time it appeared that differences were mended. As my grandmother began having children, a number of my mother's older siblings would be raised by her wealthy family "the Dowlings," which was a custom at that time in Ireland if children became economically disadvantaged by less fortunate marriages. My father's mother also grew up in such an arrangement in County Laois. Her relatives had also bequeathed my grandmother the quaint two-story home on 27 acres where my father and five of his siblings were born.

My mother's father had acquired land in a picturesque and beautiful part of Kerry outside Listowel town, in an elevated area called Banemore. He was able to build a home and also place a barn there. My mother's father "Patrick" began raising cattle along with small farming.

My mother would share how her father was successful and would bring his cattle to the market but so often his generosity and affable nature would result in the family being deprived of needed finances. He was popular and well known to pay for rounds of drinks wherever he went.

As my grandmother Bridget's health began to fail, the normal joys of childhood diminished and all of my mother's interests became subordinate to her mother's needs. Yet within that arrangement my mother found time to begin learning Irish step dancing. This became a healthy diversion from the rigors of farm life and caring for her dependent mother. It would also provide joy that would last till nearly the end of her life among family, friends and at Irish social events. Some day in her early nineties as her Parkinson's disease advanced, she would hold the back of a chair and still perform the step dancing she so loved from the time of a young girl.

After World War II my mother was in her early twenties and would travel across to England to train in nursing. Her older sister would now take over the care of her mother. As my mom was there perhaps only a short period of time, the concern for her mother grew as her health condition worsened. My mother was strong and vivacious and her sister Kathleen did not possess the same strength. My mother would leave her new adventure of living in a large city in England and return to the morose station of life on a farm to care for her invalid mother.

Perhaps in the destiny of her life it was a decision that enabled other events to confluence favorably. She would meet my father and begin a journey that would give birth to the dreams she held as a small girl. In forfeiting her life in what would appear as loss, my mother was being ushered into a life that would involve children, grandchildren and great grandchildren and where she would be cherished as the matriarch of such a large family. Her dreams and aspirations that were laid aside to care for her sick mother would still visit her life even while living in obscurity. My mother would one day vicariously guide four of her five daughters to become nurses. Her heart would be connected to that profession through her daughters in their everyday conversations with her.

Being the youngest of eleven children my mother had older siblings that had emigrated to America long before she ever knew them. An older brother Uncle Rich was first. Then followed two sisters who entered the convent in the United States. Sister Mary Richard and Sister Mary Brigetta served at an orphanage in Staten Island, New York. Then Aunt Eileen and Aunt Deliah would leave Ireland for America. My Aunt Eileen would marry a County Laois man in America who I was named after. As they would visit Ireland it was suggested by my Uncle Kieran that his nephew "William" might be interested in meeting my Aunt Eileen's younger sister, "Lily Kelliher." Through correspondence with my mother an arrangement was made for my father to travel from Dublin where he lived and worked, to Banemore, County Kerry to meet her there in her own home.

Chapter 2

Father Meets Lily Kelliher

My father worked for the Great Northern Irish Railroad at that time as a Railway Crane Man and his ability to travel would not hurt him financially as he was able to travel free of charge throughout Ireland. My father however would be picked up by my Uncle Kieran and Aunt Eileen on this occasion at the train station in Dublin where he worked and they would travel clear across the country to Banemore, County Kerry. It would have been a trip of beautiful panoramas and vistas as they traveled across to Kerry on that day.

Upon arriving that first meeting of my father and grandfather would have been very interesting to have observed. Both men were very affable and conversational and loved their country. My father would have presented himself to my mother's father as a "blue-blooded Irishman." He was carrying his fiddle in a case. He had more knowledge of Irish history and culture than most Irish people and came from a strong Irish Republican Army background. County Kerry often called the Kingdom County was regarded as a bastion of resistance to the British occupation of Ireland. My father's father as an I.R.A. soldier had spent years in prison both in England and Ireland for being part of this resistance during the early twentieth century. Such commonality would unite Irish especially those from County Kerry where Irish patriotic fervor ran high. Today's Ireland fortunately has never experienced the oppression and subjugation that previous generations suffered, and like our own forefathers of the American War of Independence, brave men had to fight for their freedom and national sovereignty against this same foreign power. My father's mother's parents would have the English show up one night and throw them all out of the house and off the land they farmed. When my great-grandfather protested, they grabbed a fiddle that hung over the fireplace and smashed it over his head and shot the dog on the floor when he barked.

As a young boy I knew my father's parents, and then as an older teenager, I stayed in their home when on vacation. My grandmother had fallen in love with my grandfather when visiting her brothers in prison in Ireland with food while they were starving. My grandfather had shared the same prison cell with them as captured I.R.A. soldiers. When finally released my grandfather would court my grandmother who was from a place in County Laois called Timahoe. He was a quiet, kind man whose ribs had been crushed by the butts of British rifles while in captivity. Despite the cruelty of his oppressors his loyalty and love for Ireland would always remain intact. He lived without any vengeance, or vitriol in his life towards those who harmed him. My father would comment years later how all people responsible for such cruelty were dead and had gone on to meet their Maker. But the sovereignty of Ireland as a free nation would always be paramount to my father, his father, and all Irish people. My father as the oldest son would always honor his father's story and valiant love for Ireland.

Understandably my father would be everything my mother's father Patrick desired for his daughter Lily. Both men having just met probably would have had one of the most satisfying experiences that day at the farm in Banemore. Each possessing that ability of being pleasant and at ease in conversation that others so often would find both attractive and enchanting. My mother would share with us as children that her father was such a sociable popular man that his funeral procession to the cemetery was considered one of the longest in the history of that area. Most of the conversation during that initial meeting was between my father and grandfather while my mother remained quiet and reticent. She would have been very occupied with the serving of that meal as my Uncle Kieran and Aunt Eileen were most likely also present. In writing this book I would love to have been a fly on the wall to hear the conversations in that quaint home that day up on Banemore hill. Despite my mother's shyness on this occasion, my grandfather's affability and my father's conversational skill caused the atmosphere of their home to become engaging and full of laughter.

From that special day forward, both my father and grandfather would form a close friendship that would last till my grandfather's death. Years later, if his name was mentioned, and my mother would say anything uncomplimentary about her father, my father would be quick to jump to my grandfather's defense, though my mother loved her father deeply, even far more than her mother. When he died my mother could not attend his funeral because she was so overcome with grief.

With my mother so adept at making meals, this certainly would have been a great Irish dinner. During all the lively and engaging conversation, my father felt very attracted to my mother's demeanor as she quietly served with competence and efficiency. She was everything my Uncle Kieran and Aunt Eileen communicated to him and even more. Despite her shyness, my father was becoming twitterpated (a term used by my wife to describe being overcome by someone from the opposite sex). One could say he was captivated, smitten, and lovestruck on that day by my mother, and that destiny was happening.

Years later my mother would comment to me how her first impression of my father was how handsome, strong, and tall he appeared as he walked through the front door of their home. This now appeared as a match made in heaven. That long awaited knight in shining armor had finally arrived to take her away from Banemore, its related sorrows and rigorous life. As my mother's sister was married to my father's uncle, this arrangement and potential match was a very typical and favored custom of the Irish people. The commonality of interests and humor with my grandfather produced a deep friendship with all lines perfectly intersecting. After dinner my father would spend time reviewing the farm with my grandfather and the many head of cattle that were grazing there. My father would stay over that night and the following day would accompany my mother to the dancehall where he would be invited to play his fiddle.

As a young attractive Irish lass growing up in County Kerry, Ireland, it would be thought that my mother should eventually meet a young man from a local town or the area in which she lived. It would seem her insular life on the farm would preclude a lot of possibilities, as it would relate to finding a suitable husband. It would not however be a man from the dance hall where her life most likely would have continued on the farm. Her destiny was to marry a man like my father, who was full of energy and motivated, and also someone who did not drink. My mother had decided even as a young girl because of members of her own family, and so many others of close association, that she would never marry a man who loved the bottle. It had been a scourge to Ireland that inflicted so much pain and suffering to families throughout the entire land. My mother's story was that she was thinking of a future family and life long before it ever happened.

My mother took control of her life in every way that she could. Her moral compass would however cause her to make decisions that seemed counterproductive to her desired future, as leaving the nursing profession in England and returning to Ireland to care for her sick mother. But as a woman of faith my mother would experience those defining moments of intervention where that needed event would reach into her world of human frailty and incapacity. Now she had just met one of the most indefatigable men in all of Ireland who would change her world beyond her most treasured dreams. The following day of my father's visit would impress him as to the industry, competence and resourcefulness of my mother. My father relished the thought of their long walk to the dancehall at Killflynn, about seven miles away. My mother was well known there for her champion Irish step dancing. She belonged to a group of young women who were called the *Dancing Darlings*. My father was also excited about participating in playing the fiddle which he had appropriately brought with him from Dublin. As my father shared with me, his only condition was that he would not be required to dance. My father would pleasantly abstain from dancing nearly all of his life yet not refrain from the humor attached to his dancing ability and lack thereof.

My father was pleased with the rich cultural heritage he would find in Kerry. It was not known by him at that time nor anyone else that he would become one of the greatest influences in advancing Irish music and culture in Ireland and throughout North America in the development of an organization that would advance Irish music, song and step dancing. My father became its founder in North America. This organization Comhaltas Ceoltoiri Eireann would one day become the foremost cultural institute of Ireland.

The following day it was decided they would walk together alone to the dancehall. My mother's father would have been very obliging to supply a *trap* which was a sporty carriage pulled by a horse or pony. The thought of a long walk together seemed far more attractive for that particular afternoon. Two young people walking together might have seemed inconsequential, but on that day but it was a surreal event, the stuff that dreams are made of. The lives of so many children, grandchildren, and great grandchildren in their loins awaited the consummation of that small event, which would result in each of them giving their lives to one another unconditionally.

My father commented as they got closer to the hall that evening that they could hear in the distance music already playing and the laughter of people inside. It was so truly Irish, and what most Irish people undeniably enjoyed. Upon arriving, my mother was treated as the belle of the ball. It wasn't until she started dancing that my father understood why. He had decided early on in the evening that he would do his best to not let this lass from Kerry be snatched away from him by anyone else. As much as my father enjoyed playing the fiddle that night, his fiddle playing ability was not comparable to my mother's talent in step dancing. These country areas of Ireland would often produce notable musicians and step dancers. My father's great talent lay dormant, its latency emerging at a future time to be a facilitator of Irish music and culture and the advancement thereof throughout the Irish world. Had he been more accomplished in playing the fiddle, his true gift may never have surfaced as a visionary for the spreading of Irish culture.

My father's gift of eloquence and Irish propriety was probably unmatched by any others he met that night. They would leave the hall with many new acquaintances made by my father. My father had a savant ability that distinguished him beyond any person I have ever met in life. He could remember people and share their stories, even many years later in life to his late nineties. He would remember the names of members of entire teams that played hurling. He could remember Irish musicians and performers that would go far back in Irish history. He could eruditely recite Irish epic and country poems, songs and long stories word for word flawlessly without falter or hesitation. He would do this never to impress but to embrace whatever was meaningful to him in his very soul. People were immensely attracted to this quality of my father because it would create endearment in every relationship, as every person is special with individual identity and purpose in life. This would one day in the land of opportunity make my father a very successful businessman. It could have been used as a tool in his chest to make money, but he used it instead to become a servant to people everywhere he went.

As they walked out that night my father would later share it was the most beautiful moon he had ever seen. Kerry had no lights on the roads, so they could walk safely in the bright light of it. It would allow them on that special night to take a few short cuts through local fields as they walked along the meandering Kerry roads on their way back to Banemore. Perhaps that moon remembered by both of my parents was a harbinger of a binding relationship that was heading towards marriage. My mother during her entire life was immensely attracted to full moons and that night it was received as a token from heaven as God's star of approval upon their life together. They walked home enthralled with each other and life despite its hardships and perplexities. They would share the rest of lives together in a journey that would span many decades of health and joy and children with those intractable sorrows that by the grace of God are often overcome. Life consists of those seminal moments that will influence things a long time to come. That night at the dance hall and the long walk together would be a quintessential part of their story that would affect many destinies and lives yet to be born.

Their seven-mile strenuous trek that could have been circumvented by using my grandfather's carriage was the better choice that evening. As a very healthy fit couple traveling under the light of a romantic moon, each of their hearts became inextricably knit to the other as they walked together hand in hand.

Dublin 1948

Chapter 3

Father and Mother in Dublin

After a couple of days my father traveled back to Dublin. It was completely on the other side of the country. It wasn't long before he corresponded with my mother and began asking her to move there. She was very desirous of such an arrangement and immediately gave her consent upon her father's approval. My father was able to locate a job with an affluent family in Dublin for my mother. They were looking to hire a young woman to cook meals and run their house. My father had shared with me that he had interviewed with a Dr. Sutton before Mother arrived to meet them. My father's strong communicative ability and affable nature would have been very helpful to break the ice before my mother's interview.

One of my mother's greatest strengths in life was the ability to multitask. Although she was very nervous about how she might perform, the doctor was impressed by my mother's energy which was always communicated to others even without words. My mother could cook, clean and perform other required services tirelessly. It was all she had known to do since she was a young girl. She got the job, and would live in a home that was far more than anything she had ever experienced. There was electricity, light switches and appliances, bathrooms and showers and other modern conveniences that were novel to my mother. She was happy with the job and performed it with energy above their expectations. Beyond serving, my mother had that innate ability to be connected with everything else that was going on, and to be intuitive about that which was not spoken. One day she would cook meals for nine children of her own and perform the tasks of motherhood with indomitable strength and energy. She was happy that she could be with my father especially on her days off. They were now completely in love. My father in honoring my mother's father sent a letter to her father thanking him for allowing my mother to live in Dublin. It would not be long however before my father was preparing to ask my mother to marry him. A bus trip to County Wicklow, south of Dublin was the perfect place. A sight overlooking "Dublin Bay" would be the spot where he would ask her the momentous question.

It turned out to be a beautiful day and everything went as planned. As they sat on a rock looking down on Dublin from the heights of the Wicklow mountains, my father posed the question to my mother. My father shared with me how in posing the question of marriage he was awestruck; in that she did not immediately answer but posed questions to him about himself and their potential future together. I asked my father what those questions were, and as lucid as my father was at ninety-seven, it was the rare moment that my father could no longer remember something. Thankfully all his stories were honest and true narratives of events that happened. My father would not share something unless he knew it to be true, and sadly my mother was no longer alive to inquire. But through past conversations with my mother, I can confidently assess with a fair degree of accuracy, the primary conditions that may have been presented to my father by my mother on that special day.

My mother was aware at least by this time that my father was devoted to Ireland. He loved his nation, and was the oldest child of a father who fought for Ireland's independence. My father was a profoundly self-educated, erudite Irishmen. He loved Irish tradition, culture, history, music, song and dance.

A serious area of cleavage existed between them that would be a game changer, and potentially altogether end their relationship. My mother was a visionary and a matriarch with destiny; her life was always defined by what would be best for her children yet to be born. She did not see Ireland at that time as a place where she wanted to raise her family, only to see them leave someday for England, America or Australia. Would my father's love for Ireland compete with his love for his wife and future children? My mother was a woman with an enlarged heart towards children that did not yet even exist. More than life itself and even to her final breath, children, grandchildren and great grandchildren were the most essential and defining part of my mother's being. Also, my father would need to promise her while raising the children together that he would never drink. These convictions would be held by my mother long before she would ever say, "I do." Any vacillation by my father on these conditions would be a deal breaker. My mother could be described as peremptory and inflexible in these two matters.

My father was to marry a woman who lived a life of strong persuasions and beliefs. There were areas of life where uncertainty did not exist. If there was ever an example of the expression *behind every great man there stands a great woman,* my mother embodied that saying.

In articulating that condition, my father never realized that in assenting to this peremptory condition, he would be fulfilling his own destiny to bring Irish culture to the North American continent in a substantial way. My father's eloquence and persuasive abilities would not be tested in changing my mother's conviction. Every major decision for the rest of their lives that connected to the welfare of the family and the running of their home would be made by my mother. She would be the moral compass that would guide our lives and faith growing up, and my father almost always would be amenable to this.

My father consented to my mother's conditions. Abstinence from alcohol presented no challenge or difficulty to my father. Such a concession, as leaving Ireland after they were married, would however be very difficult. Only his love for my mother would affect such a decision. Making such a promise, however, would not preclude Ireland from leaving my father. After emigrating to America, he would travel back again to Ireland at least 138 times.

Chapter 4

Father Moves to Kerry from Dublin

A sense of duty would call my mother again back to Banemore where her mother's condition was getting worse. Her mother was now dying, and my mother returned to Kerry to care for her, and relieve her sister Kathleen, who was now getting married. After arriving home and sharing the good news with her father, my grandfather sent a proper letter to his future son in law requesting him to consider moving to Kerry where arrangements could be made to find work and a place to settle before the wedding knot was tied.

This was a hard decision for my father in that he had a very good job with future pension on the railroad and would have to quit his job and move to Kerry and perhaps not locate something equivalent to his present job. It was again a call of destiny on his life that the love of his life, the *Dancing Darling* of Kerry, awaited him with open arms.

Before he left for Kerry to marry my mother, he was compelled to go back to his parents in County Laois. He would pay many of the creditors there that his parents owed money to, such as stores and supply houses. He insisted that nothing be discounted but that entire arrears be paid in full. He could not start a new life in Kerry and leave his parents neglected. He was the oldest of all the children and felt responsible always to take care of them. This left him practically with no money to pay for the necessary items of his own wedding. I know this would have caused my father pain as he was one of the proudest and most resourceful men I ever knew. During his life he would never be cornered, non-plussed, or lack in any situation. As a young boy I would observe this phenomenon quite often and it would create curiosity. It was as if my father always had a wind blowing on his sails. Whatever he touched turned to gold.

My grandfather was able to secure a job for my father with the Kerry Counsel where he would go out into large fields to cut bog. Bog was exploited by Ireland and other European countries as a source of fuel. These large fields are estimated to have formed over thousands of years of compressed vegetation that looks like dark soil and resembles modern-day fire logs. Ireland contained more bog than any other country in Europe. It was an excellent and inexpensive fuel for cooking and heating rooms with fireplaces.

The process of bog cutting was very unappealing to him as it involved a skill level that he found difficult at first. It would be a rare instance of my father not excelling at a physical task to be performed. In our drywall business my father's quota of sheetrock boards taped and finished was about twice the amount of the best mechanics who worked for me in later years. Only my son Sean who learned this trade from a young age would replicate his grandfather's performance and speed.

But the bog team of men were very obliging to my father. There were about 60 of them working together and my father's boss put him in charge of making tea and putting turf into sacks, to be sold and delivered throughout areas of Kerry.

Chapter 5

The Wedding of Elizabeth and William McEvoy

As time elapsed my father adjusted extremely well to a new lifestyle with different people and would make many new friends and acquaintances. But there was a wedding to plan and prepare for. My mother had a brother she was very close to whose name was Padeen, who gave money that covered some of the small items that would be needed on their wedding day. In writing it is almost an impossible thought to imagine my parents especially my father in such a place of extremity in needing to rely on anyone to provide anything necessary for life or for those connected to him. My father's Uncle Kieran in America had sent a suit that did not fit him. After it was properly tailored my father was dressed for the occasion as was my mother also. It was a temperament throughout my father's life to do the best he could in every situation, and to be content also in whatever station he found himself. The wedding day was set for February 21, 1950 at the parish church at Lixnaw, County Kerry. My father spent the previous night with my Uncle Padeen in the beautiful nearby city of Tralee.

My Uncle Padeen brought my father to the church on his tractor. It was a muddy day. He was seated at his back on a bag of hay. When they arrived, there wasn't a soul at the church. When people began arriving, they came in their work clothes and casual attire and were so friendly and joyful about the occasion. As my father would describe, "In those days people just showed up." My mother whose extended family on her mother's side were wealthy, provided a luxurious car to bring her to the church. It was her cousin who lived in Listowel. As she stepped out of his car my father was awestruck at how beautiful his bride looked. In his very words, "She was stunning." They went into the church and sat in the second row. The church began to fill with people. Neighbors, friends and many relatives were all there. Father Nicholas Browne, *a very old fashioned and saintly priest* as my father described, came out to perform the ceremony which also included an entire mass. My father had commented on how lengthy the sermon was, and how he thought it would never finish.

When it was finally over everyone gathered and embraced and shook hands. An altar boy had come out and said, "Father Browne wants to talk to both of you privately." In a small room, the priest shared with my parents in a very earnest manner about their Catholic faith and marriage and how they were not to go away to England or America, but to stay in Ireland and raise their children there.

I am sure my mother was gracious as she revered the church but that would have been one sermon that fell on deaf ears. My mother already had her sights set not on England but America and it would just be a matter of time under the right conditions that they would leave for America.

After the wedding in Lixnaw, they had stopped for drinks at the Deliah Cronin pub nearby but my father hardly touched alcohol at that time and drank lemonade instead. From there they set off to the house in Banemore. Nearly everyone headed back to celebrate with music and dance. My Uncle Padeen played the accordion and my father played the fiddle at his own wedding. A Mr. Walsh and a Mr. Johnny Cronin played also. Tables were laid out with dishes of food, soda bread, cakes and tea. After everyone had eaten, the tables were cleared to provide room for all the people to dance.

My father commented that the day was remarkably beautiful which for County Kerry was unusual as it rains there often. The music and the dancing went on through the night. My father would comment, "A turf fire was burning bright that night as the music and dancing commenced, and the sparks being knocked out of the floor."

At one point when my mother and father decided to retire, they found a man whose name was Johnny Dore drunk and sleeping in their bed, and very reluctant to leave. So, they went back out into the main room and sat by the fire the rest of the night. When he woke up the next day, they served him breakfast and he finally left.

Chapter 6

First home in Lisahan, County Kerry

So, for a period of time my father and mother would stay in Banemore. My grandfather lived there also till he died within a couple of years. My mother's mother had also died. It was during this time my father landed a new job with the Electricity Supply Board. Much of Kerry at this time was without electricity in the rural areas. A new power line connecting county Limerick with County Kerry was to be carried on poles that my father and other men were installing.

With a team of men my father placed poles throughout areas of Kerry to supply electricity to country areas of Kerry. It was during that time my grandfather became ill, and was taken to Listowel hospital where he died.

His death was eventful and tragic to my mother. He was known by everyone in their area as a most generous, friendly and affable man. Having my father was a great consolation to my mother. Her sorrow was so great that she could not attend his funeral. Mother and father were now both gone. All their children were still alive, five of them living in America.

It was around that time that my father and mother decided to purchase their first home, a small house below Banemore called Lisahan. From its back yard you could look up and see the cottage of Banemore. It was here my mother would feel freedom for the first time in her life as she was the mistress of her own home, though very small. She now had three children. My parents owned one cow also and a few chickens. My brother Patrick and I were born in Banemore house. My sister Marian was born in Listowel hospital. In Lisahan all three of us lived there with my parents. My mother would not have the convenience of any modern appliances as washing machines, dryer, refrigerator or electric stove. Everything was done by hand. My father was working hard for the E.S.B., Electric Supply Board. He would leave early every morning and come home late each day. It was while living there that my mother began directing my father towards emigrating to America. My father would have been pleased to stay in Ireland forever. All of Ireland after World War II began a slow period of development, where electricity, phones and bathrooms would become modern conveniences in homes throughout Ireland.

Strong young men like my father in his twenties would be up to the task, as Ireland was becoming a modern country. Notably in a history that my father had written in possession by my youngest sister I had just received, it could be understood in my father's remarks how much endearment he would have at that time towards fellow workers and compatriots. Wherever he worked throughout his life, even in the rigors of working as a young man on a Protestant farm, my father would keep friendships with so many people. The devoutly Christian wife of the owner of the large farm would share with my dad the harsh treatment she received from the family of her husband. She would confide with my father and share her heartache.

They would remain friends throughout all of his life till her death at the age of 100 years old. My father would comment often to me on the profound piety of her life and dedication to Christ. He would not allow any anti-Protestant sentiment to affect their friendship, despite how injurious the English had been to his own family. I personally believe my father was the lifelong beneficiary of this devout woman's pious prayers. At a future time, God would sovereignly visit our family in a very special way.

M.V. BRITANNIC

Chapter 7

Leaving for America

My father shared the story that when I was born in Banemore how he went to the midwife from the area who happened to be milking a cow. When he pressed her for the urgency, she picked up a towel and simply wiped her hands, and was off with my father for the delivery. My mother had said I was partially out by the time she arrived and she had very little to do. Everything else went well. At that time my father was working at the Electric Supply Board. After my birth my mother began thinking strategically and named me, her second born *Kieran*, after my father's uncle Kieran, who was married to my mother's older sister Eileen. In doing so they had sent a generous check, that provided money that helped buy the Lisahan house, that when later sold would pay most of the expenses incurred in going to America. With such a plan my mother was like a woman engaged on a mission as she would begin the preliminaries of preparing to emigrate to America.

At least one trip had to be made to Dublin to take care of all the legalities at the U.S. Department of Immigration. We were required to take special shots and vaccines before we were even allowed to board the ship. We all needed to have a complete medical examination to make sure we were not carrying any communicable diseases. My parents said that the whole process was expensive in terms of what it cost them to fulfill this hurdle. In selling the Lisahan house, they would be taking a risk. Had the outcome of this process been unfavorable, my parents would lose their home. It was a risk that would be accepted and even embraced at the time. My parents traveled across to Dublin with their three children to begin the formalities. They were very enamored with the Americans they would meet at the embassy. What had always been a dream to my mother was now becoming a reality.

Her reflections on America were that of a great nation like no other power on earth. They had just crushed the Nazis forces in Europe years earlier, and delivered England and Ireland from the clutches of Adolf Hitler. As a young girl my mother would hear stories that America was so rich that the streets were made out of pure gold. This exaggerated belief would be dismantled as other similar notions, yet her dream would always remain unscathed. My mother desired a future in a country that would take care of the entire family. She did not want her children to leave her at a future time and go somewhere else to find work. Since the Great Famine in the mid 1800's, Ireland was a nation that had been drained of so many of its people.

Ireland was incrementally changing however. Hundreds of years of English oppression and domination had caused Ireland to be a poor nation. As a protectorate of Great Britain over one million Irish died during the potato famine just one hundred years before I was born. The Irish were allowed to harvest only potatoes to live on, with all other produce and grains pillaged to supply the vast empire of Great Britain. It was at a time during the pinnacle of England's power and wealth under Queen Victoria that such a tragedy was allowed to take place. Ireland was like a large garden divided and owned by English landlords. England's grudging effort to mitigate suffering and starvation resulted in much Irish resentment towards Great Britain and Ireland's subjugation to its strong military power. The crises caused the greatest exodus of people in the history of mankind to leave a single island. The survivors who stayed were resolute about Irish Independence.

My father's father was among these many courageous young Irishmen who fought for Irish independence and sovereignty in the early 20th century. His parents would have educated him about this darkest period in Irish history. Thankfully after being captured, he would survive the brutal incarceration, or this story would be nonexistent with all of his posterity. At the time of this writing Ireland has now become one of the strongest economies in Europe, or in the world for that matter. Worldwide gross domestic product in 2021 was about 12,230 USD per capita. GDP in Ireland impressively reached USD 102,496.22 per capita which is substantially higher than Germany or England. The United States at 75,179 USD is also far less than that of Ireland.

Ireland's independence also was gained in 1921, only a few years after World War 1 had ended.

The Great Depression occurred only ten years later which had roiled economies throughout the world, and then during the same decade in the late 1930's Europe was plunged into World War II. Ireland as a neutral country was nevertheless affected by these events and happily survived as a strong democracy with its economy becoming progressively stronger. At the time my mother dealt with the only cards she had, and made an executive decision with the experiential knowledge she possessed back then. Though she loved her country and its culture all of her days on earth, her destiny was to become an Irish American. My father would remain however in a category of unbridled loyalty and affection to Ireland which remained the greater part of his identity in life. Neither my mother or father ever became American citizens but would remain citizens of Ireland, as also my sister Marian. At the time of these formalities my parents hardly conceived the many new connections and friends they would make in this new country. The engagement with the Americans at the embassy in Dublin was a very positive experience for both of my parents. They returned home to Lisahan with strong confidence that America would be their new home.

With the trip to the American embassy in Dublin, rite of passage was finally obtained to go to America. The home in Lisahan had been purchased for around 250 pounds, and now was to be sold for around 300 pounds. A gentleman my parents knew bought the house who was a confirmed bachelor who had the hopes that if he did marry, owning a home would be helpful in securing a bride. My parents owned this home outright. In selling this home they could now afford to buy five tickets to America on the large British ocean liner M.V. Britannic. In 1954 nearly everyone traveled by ship. There were no jet airlines but propeller aircraft, that were just being used for the first time only years earlier. The cost of flying at that time was prohibitive. My mother had owned a coat that she had loved and decided to sell it to cover incidentals for the trip. My father also gave up his overcoat.

The day was now approaching. A dream was coming true for my mother. Lisahan had been a most enjoyable home to live in. Generous neighbors like Mrs. Nolan would give my mother one quart of milk each day for the three children. Originally, they had owned a cow, which must have been sold as they were preparing to leave Ireland. My mother being the frugal person she was also arranged a yard sale in order to generate a few extra shillings to ease the financial burden of the move.

My father shared as they walked out on that particular day, how there were live ambers in the fireplace as he took his last glance. It was one of those demarcations in life that was a defining moment. Everything was about to change. A destiny was waiting for him that most men never experience. Lisahan would one day become a beautiful and elegant house purchased by an Irish contractor who would transform it magnificently. On the last trip we took to Ireland with my father and two sisters we stopped there and I told the owners we made a mistake and wanted the home back for what my parents sold it for in 1954. We all laughed heartily. The front light fixtures probably cost more than what my parents sold the entire house for when they left Ireland.

Days before my parent's departure, my father had shared the exciting news about leaving Ireland with a friend whose name was Mossy Hayes. In that same conversation Mossy had offered to drive our family to Cork where the ship was to be boarded. It was the rare person in those days who owned a car. It was a considerable blessing to my parents for such a generous offer.

As always, my father would have that inexplicable wind blowing on his back. Perhaps as a note, Ireland was a country perhaps as few in the entire world of giving people characterized by a kindly spirit. In future trips as I got older this would be an observation that I would find systemic and universal throughout the country.

The very large ship the M.V. Britannic came to a seaport town on the south coast of County Cork, Ireland from England. The ship was over 700 feet long. A considerable size ship compared to any other ocean liner at the time, smaller only than the famous Titanic by perhaps 150 ft.

Because of the size of this ship a small boat was required to ferry passengers a half mile out to this large vessel. It would have been a breathtaking sight to my parents when they arrived at Cobh to see that ship, sitting out in the harbor. My father shared about the somber peal of the bells of nearby Shandon on the river Lee that seemed to mark the solemnity of that day. There would be the heartbreaking scene of so many Irish families saying good-bye to their loved ones, and the waving of colored handkerchiefs as the smaller vessel carrying passengers pulled away from the dock to transport everyone out to the larger ship. With the deep droning blast sounding from the large ship, the time had finally come for departure.

My father described such a universal occurrence as this as part of the scourge of emigration that was all too familiar to so many Irish.

As a family we would be staying in the least expensive quarters on the ship, but it would be an experience that neither one of my parents would ever forget, as it was a defining moment for their future. Their home and nearly all of their belongings were sold. All that we now possessed as a family was placed in a trunk that could easily fit in the back of a car. Boarding the ship brought with it the irrevocable reality that they were starting a new life. Their lives would never be the same.

The ship had been used in transporting troops in World War II just years earlier. It was refitted back to a regular passenger ocean liner. The meals served on board were a great novelty to my parents. It was July 3, 1954. They would be arriving in New York City harbor one week later on July 10.

As my father looked east long after the ship left port, he would remember seeing the beautiful Kerry mountains in the distance. His heart would throb as they passed the coasts of Kerry and then Dingle harbor. Where he stood was entirely because of the promise he made to my mother that he would leave Ireland and take her to America. They would raise their children there. Now he wondered would he ever be able to return? It wouldn't be until later that day that the final vestige of mountains could still be seen from the Blasket Islands, the most westerly European archipelago of islands off County Kerry. It's difficult to imagine this decision and what it meant to my parents, but especially my father. All that mattered to him was left behind with the exception of his wife and children. He truly loved Ireland. It was his home.

One of the things I admired greatly about my parents was their ability to take thoughts, feelings and experiences that seem to conflict and cause sorrow, yet still allow competing areas and unrelated events to stand on their own merits, to the extent of even embracing the new event, without losing any the old. At the time of this writing in Tennessee I have not been able to do this although we live in such a beautiful home. My father could compartmentalize life better than anyone I ever knew. This ability helped both of my parents to make important decisions despite the related risks. They did not look at life in the rear-view mirror but constantly pressed forward and embraced their future together.

During the week-long voyage across the North Atlantic my parents would be up on the ship's deck meeting so many new people. My father often brought his fiddle and would play for my mother while she step-danced. Nearly everyone on the ship enjoyed this immensely during their voyage to New York. So many passengers on the ship looked forward each day to being entertained by my parents. Many would dote over my infant sister Marian. A well-known French actress who was among the passengers would come down to the cabin every night to kiss Marian.

As the ship got closer to destination one of the overriding thoughts of my parents was that of a mission accomplished. With all of the legalities in order, and all of the necessary monies paid out for different things related to the trip, there was little money left which greatly concerned them. My Uncle Kieran and Aunt Eileen were to meet my parents at the pier in New York harbor, but my parents were incredibly proud and would be very ashamed to not have enough money to keep them until my father found work in Suffolk County, Long Island, New York where we were going. A very eventful thing happened before we would even arrive at the pier. As children we would hear about this event to make us aware of the goodness of God to the lives of my parents.

One night before arriving in New York a knock came on the cabin door which startled both of my parents. To their surprise, the captain of the ship was standing outside the door smiling. My parents were awestruck. On such a large ocean liner only the highest-class passengers might have the honor of the captain sitting in their company at a meal. He had a white envelope in his hand. He explained how the passengers on the ship had taken a collection in appreciation for all the entertainment during the voyage. My parents were in disbelief. When the door had closed my parents were like school children as they counted the money. It would take them far along in New York and allow them not to be a burden to our relatives there.

I can hardly recount a time in my parent's lives where they would be cornered or non-plussed. There would always seem to be a special hand of Providence that would reach down into their lives and make a way through almost every situation and difficulty.

My father described the eventful day of arriving in New York harbor. The first sight of New York was spectacular as the tall buildings were seen brimming over the horizon. How many hundreds of thousands of Irish had shared this same experience entering New York harbor with the shining beacon of the Statue of Liberty greeting them. "Give me your tired, your poor, your huddled masses yearning to breathe free..."

My parents as so many other Irish and people from other nations were embracing the destiny that this nation as no other nation could provide to those who had a desire to succeed. A nation where possibilities were limitless to the person who desired to achieve.

List of
PASSENGERS

M.V.
"BRITANNIC"

JULY 2ND, 1954

TOURIST

—

LIVERPOOL
COBH
NEW YORK

CUNARD LINE

Chapter 8

Arriving in America

My father would share that on the day they arrived at Pier 37 was a day of unbearable heat. It was July 10, 1954. Such temperatures they never experienced at home. Ireland has a moderate climate with not too cold winters and summers not extremely hot. My father would comment that processing all immigration documents went very smoothly. As the passengers disembarked the ocean liner a long gangway was the final off-ramp for the passengers as they stepped off the ship. There was a line on the ground with a gentleman standing on the far side with his hand stretched out, "You are very welcome to the United States of America." My father reached out to shake that hand as he stepped over the line. He often shared that story as the most defining moment for both he and my mother, that they were now part of the American story. They had no idea of what their future would hold for them in the United States.

Their story as with so many others involved risk, but it would be a risk embraced, and placed into the hands of God. My parents possessed that unique gift of adaptability that would enable them to overcome immediately the culture shock of a new country. Besides there would be plenty of Irish everywhere in this new land. My father would be marked by a destiny as he stepped off that plank of bringing traditional Irish music and talent to the United States as perhaps few others would ever accomplish as the founder of Comhaltas Ceoltoiri Eireann for North America. This organization would one day become the foremost cultural institute of Ireland that would also facilitate Irish culture and music reaching Irish people interspersed throughout the United States and Canada. My father's enduring gift in leaving Ireland was to bring Ireland to nearly everyone he would meet in

America. Many Americans would be enamored by his unapologetic Irishness, and the great honor in which he would conduct his affairs.

Perhaps the first trial now awaited my parents when they disembarked. It was my Uncle Kieran and Aunt Eileen. They were nowhere to be found on that particular day. And when finally found, my parents could sense them as being unreceptive, even cold. From New York City harbor to New Hyde Park on Long Island was not an especially long distance. It was where Uncle Kieran and Aunt Eileen lived, and where we were to stay that first night. They had a second home further out on Long Island in Suffolk County in a place called Centereach, where we were to live for a while and rent from them. The trip to New Hyde Park would travel through areas of New York City and Queens that brought profound revelation to my mother that America also had poverty and hardship. So much had seemed very dirty, shabby and opposite to my mother's thoughts of grandeur of what she imagined America to be. As a young girl she had been told the streets of America were paved with gold. Ireland was a very clean country. Beautiful villages and small towns and breathtaking landscapes were everywhere to be found. Ireland was perhaps the friendliest, most inviting nation on earth. People were never too busy and always willing to help. New York seemed to be bustling and busy place.

Whatever the initial perception, it was here, for better or worse, my mother decided opportunity was to be found. And she would raise her children in a place where they would be inclined to stay and someday raise their own families. My mother always relished the thought of having many grandchildren near her. Now on that trip to New Hyde Park, as uncomfortable and perplexed as both of my parents felt, my father would have exercised the highest level of propriety and kindness. Affability and cheer in conversation goes a long way towards dissipating conflict.

When arriving at their New Hyde Park home my parents remained outside waiting, and decided to go over just a couple of doors to my mother's other sister Deliah where it was decided that we would stay for the night. My Aunt Deliah and Uncle Bill Nielson were gracious people and made my parents feel very welcome and at ease. Their son Bill would one day become a very close part of our immediate family.

Chapter 9

Centereach, Long Island, N.Y.

It was Saturday, July 10, 1954. Sunday my parents attended Mass at the Church of the Holy Spirit in New Hyde Park and after service they headed out east on Long Island to Centereach in Suffolk County. This was a small ranch type home owned by Uncle Kieran and Aunt Eileen. The drive would be a bit longer to get out there.

Upon arriving my parents were met with the most pleasant surprise. As they stopped outside the home on Cedar Lane, a banner had been placed above the door which read "Welcome Home." The neighbors had heard that an Irish family was moving in and had all gotten together to give our family a warm reception. This was extremely heartwarming to my parents. Most Americans had a great affinity towards the Irish and were enamored by the way they spoke and their friendly spirit. The small country of Ireland and the emigration of its people to the new world would probably be among the greatest contributions to America's greatness in the world. Irish people thrive under freedom. At the time of this writing one half of all United States presidents can trace their lineage back to Ireland. Joe Biden (46th President) can trace his ancestry back to counties Louth and County Mayo. One could say the great Irish diaspora to the United States has substantially affected the entire world by providing the great Presidents, leaders, and notable people to fill positions that would influence the peace and prosperity of the entire world, to fight against tyranny and oppression.

As my parents were converged upon by these friendly Americans, one of the neighbors, the McDonald's had invited my mom and dad and others over for coffee, tea and cake, which my parents were very obliged. While sitting at the table my parents were introduced for the first time to a "tea bag" which to their knowledge didn't exist in Ireland.

They didn't know what to do with it, so my father quietly suggested to my mother to watch what everyone else did with theirs. In Ireland, where people drink a lot of tea, only loose tea was ever made. And in the whole world, except England, Ireland has the finest tea. My parents shared with us the joy of that day. Just a week earlier they were in a different part of the world among their own people and friends. Now they were with people they had never met, yet they could not have felt more accepted and at home.

The great blessing of the new world to the Irish for centuries was that they spoke English. Forced by centuries of English oppression and occupation, the language spoken by Irish people became English rather than Gaelic, the native language of Ireland, which is still spoken by many Irish living in traditional areas of the country.

Both of my parents were excellent conversationalist, and enjoyed hearty humor and laughter. They became friends with the entire street in a short amount of time. My father talked about this event before his death as if it happened yesterday. There were the Kings across the road. The Loughlins next door, and the McDonalds a couple of doors over. Friendships would continue even long after my parents moved to their own purchased home.

It appeared to my father and mother in very short order that my Aunt Eileen and Uncle Kieran were very idiosyncratic people. My Uncle Kieran decided that he would stay often out at Cedar Street in Centereach to watch his home that it would not become damaged. He would show hypersensitive behavior towards many things. My parents chose to honor them. It was they who sent a generous check to purchase the Lisahan house they sold to come to America. They also were our sponsors that enabled us to live in the United States.

Chapter 10

First Job–Oscar Eilerston

And one of the most important contributions to my parents was Uncle Kieran providing my father his first contact for his first job in the United States. When my father was loaned a bicycle to ride to his first job many miles away, he signed a contract to return the property in the condition it was originally loaned.

Such behavior would motivate my parents to find their own home as soon as possible. But how could such an event happen? The only money they possessed was the money they received from the captain of the ship before arriving in New York. In paying their expenses thus far, they had been spared from a great loss of dignity which both of them had possessed, and that would always remain a part of their lives.

My father's congenial manner with people would smooth over any potential conflicts that would ordinarily erupt in such situations. My father through life had great deference towards his father and his father's family, and in later years would often visit and correspond with all of his relatives from his father's side in Ireland, who were as in my mother's words when speaking of splendid Irish persons, *the cream of Ireland.*

The next day was Monday July 11th and my father would meet his first employer, a man by the name of Oscar Eilerston from Denmark. He lived by a large lake which attracted a lot of tourism and summer residents from New York City called Lake Ronkonkoma. He was a businessman and owned a lot of real estate all over Long Island, and needed a strong man to do new construction and upkeep on all of his properties. Many of the homes were two-bedroom cottages.

Getting up early that morning, in a new country, there would be no offer to drive my father on the first day even though a car was available. My father rode the loaner bike and became very lost on his first day trying to find the large 53 room Copenhagen Hotel situated on the lake at Lake Ronkonkoma. As he would ask for directions from people he met along the way, nearly all of them could not understand him. Perhaps an Irishman trying to pronounce the Indian words *Lake Ronkonkoma* for the first time would be hard to communicate to others. My father felt sorrowful on that first day for being late, but Oscar and Olga Eilerston were very sympathetic and understanding. As Europeans they were very favorable to the Irish. From the day my father first met them, a strong bond of loyalty, trust and friendship occurred between them. Both Olga and Oscar would make a determined effort to see my father do well in the United States. My father would serve Oscar with indomitable energy. On his first day my father cleaned windows on the large hotel. In storytelling, my father would later say, "Of which there was no scarcity." In addition to the large hotel, the Eilerstons also owned 22 summer bungalows, of which my father said, "He bought and sold continually."

In no time my father graduated to digging and building cesspools and painting new homes. When a cesspool would be installed in one of the new homes my father would dig it by hand, lay all the blocks and backfill it, all in one day. One day as my father stood deep in a cesspool hole he had dug, a large brick went whizzing past his head. The man on top was mentally challenged and threw the stone without signal as had been agreed. My father could have lost his life that day or the ability to ever work again. This book would have told a different story. Many precious descendants would never have been born. How we need to live lives connected to Divine approbation and intervention. I often contemplate in my own life that I have also been mercifully spared from tragedy a number times over the years.

As the only son who worked with my father in our family drywall business, I personally observed over so many years the traits that endeared my father to Olga and Oscar Eilerston and to so many others he would later be connected to. As a family business performing over 12,000 jobs in over 60 years, we never experienced an official complaint or had litigation against our business. My father never wrote out a contract for any customer to sign, but only a written proposal designating what we were to perform that he would sign. Every job was transacted with a handshake. My father's very core was to be fair and honest in every transaction with people. As a young man in my teens, I was working on one of my father's jobs and I ran the entire project. Just a short time into the job I had come to the realization that the woman we were working for was not all there. The woman had cats that lived with her that were so many that it was clear something was wrong. On the final day as the job was being finished, I simply mentioned that my father was coming by for payment. The woman immediately erupted into laughter, and I knew my father was certainly in trouble on this particular job. When my father arrived for payment, I communicated my concern which was very ascertainable by the woman's behavior. My father quietly told me to place my tools in the truck and politely bid the woman good bye as we left together. As we drove away my father made no comment or complaint. It was a mistake and it would serve no purpose to even discuss what had just happened.

Often, we worked for young couples who were just starting out in life. My father would often tell them at the end of the job to send the money whenever they had it. I would question my father later on after we left the job about such a policy. My father affirmed to me that he always received payment in these instances. Inwardly I balked at a policy marked by such honest simplicity that frankly bordered on naivety. He was however in reality utterly free from any greed for wealth or material gain in running his business. This is why people loved my father. He had benefactors as the Eilerstons, and never forgot those kindnesses in life where he was the recipient. This trait didn't diminish his ability to successfully run a business. He was one of the sharpest businessmen I ever knew, and could be very decisive, especially when dealing with bad players or any form of dishonesty.

One time a young man from Ireland had stayed at our home for a period of time. He had cashed a bad check at the same bank of my parents and the teller knowing his connection to my parents cashed the check, and in the outcome wound up losing her job. My father hearing the story went to the branch and implored the branch manager for the teller to be reinstated. My father paid for the entire amount of the bad check. Days later my mother confronted the young man. He was staying in an adjoining room next to my own. As the conversation evolved, I could hear things breaking in the room. As mentioned, my mother was the strongest woman I ever knew, and one could say she took matters into her own hands. My parents' reputation was assailed because of that person. They were unaware of his dishonesty and were resolute in having him leave our home. Weeks later the F.B.I. would show up at our door looking for him.

My father's industry, honesty and fairness commended him to the Eilerstons over the entire course of his employment with them. As the first day for my father came and went, weeks and months would follow. My father would now become very familiar with Long Island especially areas throughout Suffolk County. Oscar and Olga Eilerston were like a gift to him from heaven and the relationship was very reciprocal. Other than that first day, my father never once again arrived late or took a sick day while working for them. During that time my father would have such great joy riding his bike home to Cedar Street, Centereach each day. He was now paying all bills and expenses to keep his family in this new country.

Chapter 11

Wiggins Street, Lake Ronkonkoma

My mother was in a special trial with her sister and my father's uncle back in the Centereach home. My mother was overwhelmed with the degree of carefulness needed to live in such an arrangement of hyper scrutiny, especially with three children. This would be communicated to my father. My earliest memory in life, being barely two years old, was not to press against a screen on the back door that my Uncle Kieran was concerned about in case it would be bulging out and not flat. My father understood and would encourage my mother to hold on for the time. The pain and difficulty of living in his uncle's home would hopefully be a temporary experience. They were to honor their relatives from Ireland although it proved unbearable to my mother.

Throughout my life I always regarded my mother's sincere and simple faith as the archetype of what I wanted for my own life. I don't ever remember questioning the holy doctrine of Christ, as the only begotten of the Father. My mother was the one who taught us everything about our faith and communicated it so well. My father was the enforcer, like we'd never miss Mass, the Sacraments or the Holy Days of Obligation. But my mother embodied the heart of our faith, as was the experience of many families, especially Irish. As a young boy I can remember singing to Jesus songs I had learned as I was outside playing. But I was always intrigued by my father, as I knew he did not possess what my mother had, yet there was a something profound on his life that would constantly overcome the many hard and difficult equations hurled by life. I would observe this throughout the years, especially in the many years of being personally involved in business together. It would not be until many years later that this phenomenon was understood and the curtain was rolled back for me to see clearly what was behind it. This I will share a little later on in their story.

One of those events that required such intervention was about to take place. That blessing and favor, that is often worth more than gold, was about to visit my parents again. With my father's heart burdened by the difficulty of Cedar St. in Centereach, he asked Mr. Eilerston one day just how one would ever go about purchasing a home and what it would require, and how much money would be needed?

At the time my father posed the question, they had absolutely no money except that which was necessary to pay current bills. When Mr. Eilerston did not answer, my father in politeness did not press the matter any further, as this would clearly fit under the category of a hopeless cause, that even Mr. Eilerston himself could not answer. At the end of the week as was custom, my father went into the office to receive his paycheck from Mrs. Eilerston. On that particular Friday Olga asked him to stay a little longer as she had a matter to discuss with him. Her tone had initially concerned him as it expressed a seriousness that he could see in her countenance as she spoke. Had my father violated any propriety in asking her husband that question during the week? He would never again breach his relationship with such a fine man as Mr. Eilerston by allowing himself such familiarity with his boss.

Mrs. Eilerston in seeing my father's concern at her professional manner asked my father to sit down on the chair and said, "Bill, Oscar and I would like to make a proposal to you about selling a house to you and Lily for your family." My father being taken back commented how he did not have any money. Mrs. Eilerston abruptly stopped my father by saying, "Bill, I didn't mention anything about money, did I?" As she proceeded, she mentioned a charming small home in a pleasant neighborhood in Lake Ronkonkoma on Wiggens Street. The house would come with furniture, appliances, beds, kitchen silverware, dishes and plates etc. The home would be titled to my parents and a small deduction of $60.76 per month would be taken from his paycheck each week to pay the mortgage which they would hold for them. There would only be a $50.00 down payment. They had only been in America a matter of months, less than a year, and they would now be owning their own home.

My father would have peddled home very fast on that particular Friday to announce such good news to his Lily. It would far exceed their wildest dreams that he and my mother were about to own their first home. My mother was overtaken with happiness she had never known. She would now be the mistress of her own home as she was in Lisahan when she had left Ireland.

"God has been so good!" My mother's declaration for answered prayers. She had held her peace in submission to my father's advice in protecting a relationship that honored his father's brother, that would hopefully be mended one day. At present it had been severely damaged. In a very short time, they would be preparing for the big move. By the time they moved another profound event was to take place. Without my father being aware, my mother had been able to put aside a small amount of money on the meager salary of my father to purchase a car. The ability to save was one of my mother's greatest attributes throughout her life. Somehow through their small circle of friends and acquaintances my mother found an inexpensive car for my father to drive to work. My father had shared a story with me many years ago of how before they had a vehicle, he would take a short cut across Lake Ronkonkoma during freezing weather by riding his bike across on the ice. On particular days he would hear the ice cracking. This would cause great concern to my mother. Driving to work especially during brutally cold Long Island winters was now such a convenience. This would be the first automobile they ever owned and would substantially change their world. It was a 1930's clunker but would serve them well for the time. A new home and a car to drive our family was beyond the expectations of my parents being such a short time in the new country.

With such wonderful news as owning their first home it was supposed by both of my parents that Uncle Kieran and Aunt Eileen would be very happy. They would not have to be concerned any more about their home and something being damaged by one of the children. It was not to be, however. They did not celebrate this event in the lives of my parents. Harsh words were spoken to my mother by her sister that would later be hard to retract. Time alone would heal wounds and relationships would be restored. Uncle Kieran years later would call my father and offer to watch all of us children with his wife so that my parents could travel to Ireland together. With nine children to watch this would have been a job hardly anyone should volunteer for. It would have been easier to watch and take care of wild

Indians. It was exceptionally thoughtful and generous gesture to both of my parents and brought an olive branch that mended wounds on every side. Years later I would reflect with sorrow on poor Aunt Eileen and Uncle Kieran on how difficult it must have been to watch all of us at that time in their older years. It clearly showed how desirous they were to restore their relationship with my parents. After Uncle Kieran died my mother and Aunt Eileen shared a close friendship for many years until my aunt's death.

On the day of our move to the new home in Lake Ronkonkoma there was not much to do. My parents simply drove their car to the new home. Everything was there for them. It was like a scene from the movie *It's a Wonderful Life*. Mrs. Eilerston had personally taken special care to make the home completely ready for us. I remember the day we moved in; I was not yet three years old.

In the writing of my parent's story, I am reflective how nearly all of the interconnected people in the lives of my parents are gone, how only in this world we get a chance to be good to people and to love others unconditionally. The importance of forgiveness and not allowing any bitter root ever to defile our lives. Connecting our lives by faith to Christ and His efficacious work and serving others is the only thing we will meet someday in heaven. That God would have placed people with such beautiful enlarged hearts as Oscar and Olga Eilerston at such a critical juncture in the lives of mom and dad was a cordial of grace bestowed upon my young parents. Only angels met unaware could have ever been so kind to them.

My life at Wiggens Street represents that time where memories flood my mind in technicolor. Before Wiggens Street memories are very spotty and few, as I was also very young. But one of the first things my parents resolved to do was to find the closest Roman Catholic Church. The nearest church to our residence was St. Joseph's in Lake Ronkonkoma. It became our parish and all nine children would attend the grammar school there. On our first Sunday, my parents saw an elderly woman walking along the main road on the way to church and my father pulled over and offered her a ride. She happened to be from County Clare, Ireland. She was also walking to attend mass at St. Joseph's. Mrs. Kennedy, a widow, became one of my mother's closest friends. She became the Irish mother my mother never had. As children Mrs. Kennedy would often come over to babysit. She was a grandmother to us. As Mrs. Kennedy became older my mother would constantly visit, call and stay in touch nearly every day even as our family substantially grew. My mother possessed the attribute of being a very loyal friend to those she knew and loved throughout her entire life.

My father would continue with the Eilerstons. On harsh winter days my father would be home but never idle. On such days he would shovel the sidewalks at the nearby village of Lake Ronkonkoma. My mother would take care of the children at home and our new house would become a sanctuary of joy to our lives. At the age of four I met my best friend, Harry Swanson. His mother would also become one of my mother's closest lifelong friends.

Wiggins Street was a location that fit our lives perfectly as a starter home. It was very near the largest fresh water lake on Long Island called Lake Ronkonkoma. We were also able to walk to the nearby village in a matter of minutes. My mother walked us to the lake several times per week during the summer. Walking alongside that carriage and listening to my mother's loving conversations are among the best memories I have growing up as a child. We are hardly shaped by those things in life that are formal, intentional or academically taught. Those things are easily lost by competing thoughts from others. But the love of a mother and its intrinsic value to our lives shapes the very people we become and what God by His design has made us to be. My mother carried this love to her children her entire life. Before she died, I would often communicate this to her when she visited my home each week.

My father while working for Mr. Eilerston often encountered other trades that worked on the many homes Mr. Eilerston owned throughout Suffolk County. One of the trades my father found interesting was drywall. The drywall people installed sheetrock and finished walls, making them ready for paint. During lunch breaks and after work my father spent time trying to learn the skill of spackling (plastering). Every chance he had, he would practice the techniques and process of *spackling and taping* as it is called. The drywall people he met were very helpful and friendly. Neither my father nor any of them could foresee or ever contemplate that this poor immigrant they were helping would one day start a family drywall business that would accomplish over 12,000 jobs throughout Long Island over the course of many decades. It was a great joy to share in my father's business as we worked in tandem together for nearly forty years. My father had the ability in life to connect with people who were often attracted to his energy and engaging conversation. His unapologetic Irishness charmed nearly all our American customers.

The skill level and dexterity my father had in this trade was something that could hardly be found anywhere in the industry. People were mesmerized as they watched his tools slide and glide over walls as he whistled the tunes of Irish music as he worked. His indefatigable strength and pace were assuaged only by the offer of an obliging customer for a break to have some tea. As a young teenager, I quietly sat and listened to the light engagement between customer and contractor. Just moments before a frenetic pace of seeming unalterable energy was being expended to get the job done. Now that paramount bond was formed that would result in a loyal customer with unswerving allegiance to our family business. At the time of this writing a customer from over forty years ago who used my father called. As I am also heading to New York from my retirement in Tennessee to visit my son and his family I will be doing this small repair for our customer. It provides that nostalgic therapy of a sentimental return to that which is irrecoverable. To visit that home where I can almost once again hear my father's voice and distinctive whistling in a place where we once worked together.

The post war period of United States was a consequential time for many immigrants. Long Island, New York where my parents settled was a beautiful long island jutting off New York City with perhaps the most beautiful white sand beaches found anywhere in the world. It became one of the fastest growing areas for construction in the United States. A mass exodus of millions of people would leave New York City for the *suburbs* after World War II. New York City and its thriving economy had a great impact on the economy of Long Island. Young soldiers who came back from fighting World War II were buying homes with government secured loans. My parents' timing and the place they chose could not have been more strategic to raise a family and build their lives.

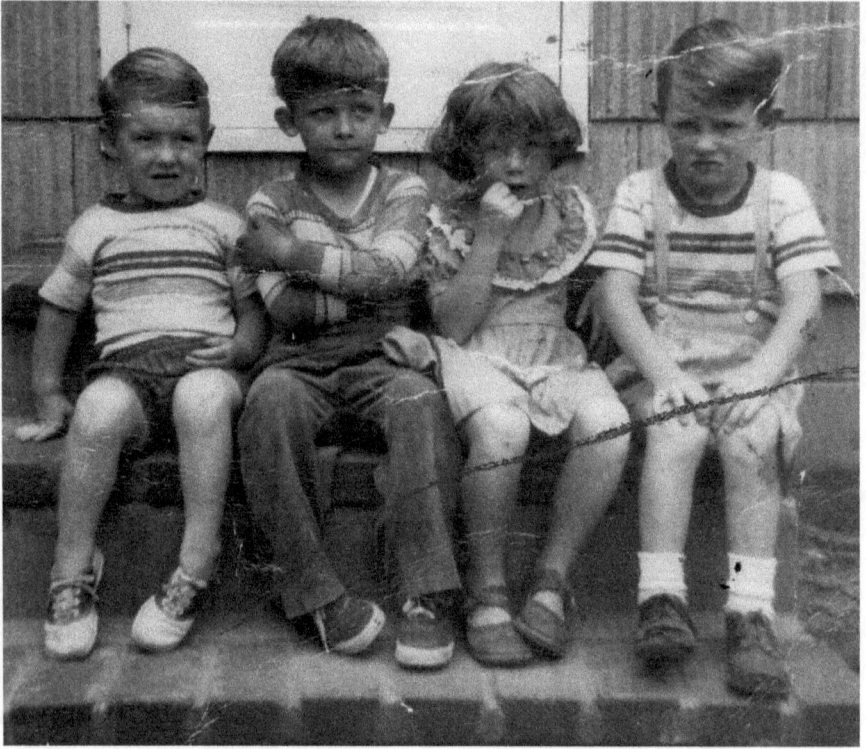

Chapter 12

Childhood at Wiggins Street

My mother would hold the fort while my father worked. As children we enjoyed a most devoted high-spirited mother who made our lives as happy as any child could ever experience. Having breakfast each morning was either porridge or eggs and toast. We especially loved the mornings my mother would make hard boiled eggs. My mother would place our eggs in an egg stand and then carefully cut off the top of each of our eggs so we could eat them with a small spoon. Often after we finished eating our eggs and our mother wasn't looking, we would reverse the eggs in the egg stand with the cut side facing down so it would look like a boiled egg not yet eaten. We would call out to our mother. "Hey mom, you forgot to cut our gug-gug" (our word for eggs). When my mother would come into the kitchen and cut the top of the empty egg and act upset, we would laugh hysterically as she would chase us into another room and tickle us for fooling her. We would play this joke over and over, and my mother would play along each time as if it had never happened before. Inside our home was a mother so full of love and acceptance. When I think back upon our childhood, I am mindful of such beautiful attributes of a mother as my own who inherently possessed such an ability to love without having been damaged by her own difficult and strenuous life and childhood.

As a young boy barely three my older brother and I would love to play *bronco* by jumping on my mother's back and riding her like a wild horse. One day after playing for a while my mother sat up on the floor and said, "I wonder when you grow up someday will you remember me playing with you like this?" Both my brother and I wrapped our arms around her neck exclaiming, "Mom, we will never forget you playing with us, we will always remember."

I am grateful to have possessed that ability in life to remember back to when I was barely two and three years old, because I am solaced by such memories. As a very young boy I can remember playing with my brother outside in the front yard. We were throwing paint sticks in the air that would glide by rapidly flipping on the way down to the ground. I can still see my mother watching us from the window so intrigued by our game. When we came inside, she placed dollar bills in our hand and told us to buy whatever toy we liked at Yarlow's five and ten cent store in the village nearby. Those moments in life are still remembered of a mother's tender love and infatuation towards her children. I am also comforted that I saw my mother every night for a period of years before she died. I would often come home late from our drywall business, eat a quick dinner and head off to see my parents. As I drove to their home, I would often sense in my own heart that sweet intonation of God's love that often directs our steps without the corresponding voice we desire to hear. While my mother was still alive, my father and I found our engagement talking about business and customers. I enjoyed hearing his advice. He always had the most simplistic answers to the most challenging problems because my father resolved business problems by communicating with people in a way that prevented alienation and estrangement.

Something the younger siblings in our family did not experience was my mother's great ability to tell stories. Every night I couldn't wait to go to bed. "What new story was Mom going to tell us tonight?" One night my mother shared with us a story of her life while she lived in Dublin after she had met my father. The story would have us in inconsolable laughter. The couple my mother worked for were very wealthy. The husband was a distinguished doctor and they often entertained notable people from Dublin. My mother being a country girl from County Kerry from the opposite side of Ireland was constantly grilled by the wife on etiquette and manners. On the night of a very formal dinner, the doctor's wife rehearsed with my mother that when she served dinner she was to only say "yes ma'am or no ma'am" when spoken to. My mother shared with us how when she brought a duck dinner into the dining room with all the distinguished guests, she laid the duck on the table and quipped, "Yes ma'am, no ma'am, yes if you please, up the duck's (blank) I stick the green peas."

As children, we were hysterical at my mother's funny quips and anecdotal stories. She had so many funny one-liners often taken from her father who she loved. My mother would often say if we were idle, "You have nothing to do, and all day to do it." If we asked my mother "What's for dinner," or "What's for lunch?" we often got the answer, "Frogs croak and Kerrog's buttermilk." If we took too long to do something, Mother would say, "You're as slow as a hedgehog."

Some stories we so enjoyed we would ask my mother to share over and over again. Many stories were from folklore of Ireland. Stories of giants, banshees, leprechauns and other legends. Often my mother would just conjure up from her own imagination and she would keep us spellbound to hear the rest of the story the following night. She would share a condensed tongue twister from Carolyn Wells about Betty Botter "Who bought a bit of butter, but the butter was too bitter, so Betty Botter bought another bit of butter!"

When we were very young my mother would sing to us a funny story of a young handsome man who mistakenly married a woman who was ninety and not nineteen, as he had supposed. It would start off, "Oh the first night I married I ne'er slept a wink..." The song would go on to describe the wedding night and the supposed young bride taking out her teeth, removing a wig and exposing a bald head as we laughed hysterically my mother would sing "She took off her left leg and threw it at me..." The song would proceed until he finally realized that she wasn't nineteen, but ninety years old. The lyrics would end, "Oh wasn't she charming for nineteen years old!" The animation of my mother's voice, her wit, humor and Kerry accent made us want to hear that song over and over again.

I often wondered how my mother's temperament and buoyancy, her continual joy and lightheartedness could have been so much a part of her person considering the hardships of her life in Ireland. As I pulled up to my parent's house on a Sunday afternoon before my mother's death, she stood out at the end of her walkway as she waited for me. As I swung the car around in her driveway to allow her to get in on the passenger side, I could see my mom so elderly, so lovingly waiting for me. I reflected how someday she'd be gone and how very important every moment was. She was a mother who throughout life epitomized everything God created a mother to be.

When my mother told us about Banshees, we were so frightened by them. They were small women with long hair and a comb who would foretell the death of a person by crying and lamenting outside the home of the person three days before they died. In Ireland banshees were believed to warn only families of pure Irish descent and those who had certain name patterns. Those whose last names consisted of the M's, the E's and the O's (McEvoy) were among those to be visited. The Banshee stays with the family and their descendants even if they lose their position in society or reduced to the ranks of the poor. Well, as children if we heard a dog howling at night we were up and out of our bedrooms and into our mother for solace and protection as we looked at each other and wondered which one of us was marked by the howl. I lamented as a young boy that we had such a sequence of letters in our last name. Maybe somehow the banshees would stay busy in Ireland and not come to America and bother us.

When I was twelve years old, we visited Ireland as a family. At a particular member of my father's family, we stayed at a farm house that had a large field of stalks that were very high. I found it beyond enchanting to go out into these stalks like a Ninja where no-one could ever find you. One afternoon my mother and my older brother Patrick were together at the clothes line. It was a perfect scenario to pull a *Banshee*. I let out an incredible crying scream cusping my hands on either side of my face. My brother was terrified at the supposed Banshee. I had to stop as I could not control my laughing. It was the only event in our lives as brothers that I was not at the hard end of his cruel humor. He never to this day knew the true story. I let him sweat it out the next few days to know if he was the one the Banshee came to visit.

The stories of leprechauns were far more enjoyable. Small bearded men, wearing a coat and a hat who were full of mischief and wit. Often, they were found to be working on small shoes. If caught, they could be demanded of the pot of gold that every leprechaun held in possession. These small fairy men also possessed what a lot of Irish always have nearby, called a *cruiscin* or a jug to drink from. It was always next to them as they worked their trade and hammered their shoes, they would hold the jug up to their mouths and drink.

My mother had a song she often sang to us as little children, about a leprechaun that was caught one night. As the story goes, if you took your eyes off the leprechaun for even a split second, he would vanish and you would lose your hoped-for pot of gold. The leprechaun, full of mischief would always outwit the captor by deceiving him into taking his eyes off him for just the smallest moment and the leprechaun would disappear out of sight along with the pot of gold.

Like it was yesterday, I can remember that song of at least sixty-five years ago. I was only four years old and it was an often-repeated story and song I could never forget. As a small boy I was so intrigued by leprechauns and always wanted to catch one. He'd never get to fool me like he did to the guy in that song!

"In a shady nook one moonlit night, I spied a leprechaun.
With scarlet cap and a coat of green, and a cruiscin by his side,
Twas tick tack tick his hammer went, upon a weeny shoe.
And I laughed to think of a purse of gold, but the fairy was laughing too!
With tip toe step and a beating heart quiet softly, I drew nigh.
There was mischief in his merry face, a twinkle in his eye.
He hammered and sang with tiny voice, and drank his mountain dew.
And I laughed to think he was caught at last, but the fairy was laughing too!
As quick as thought I seized the elf, give me your purse I cried!
The purse says he, tis in her hand, that lady by your side!
I turned to look; the elf was gone! Now what was I to do?
O I laughed to think what a fool I'd been, but the fairy was laughing too!"

I am sure this obscure Irish song written in the late 1800's around the time when my mother's parents were young, was sung to her by her father when she was a small girl. It would have fit my grandfather Patrick's persona and humor. It is why everyone loved him.

Though Irish folklore being just mere superstition, my mother would share with us the orthodoxy of our faith that we embraced as completely true. How St. Patrick went to Ireland when we were pagans and hedonistic. How in using the shamrock which became a symbol of Ireland he would explain the great Christian doctrine of the Holy Trinity. That the metaphor of this small sprig with three leaves, yet one plant would help the Irish people to understand the Christian faith and the divinity of Christ as the eternal Son of God.

As children, even very small, we were made to understand in a very profound and beautiful way such a central doctrine of our faith. We were taught how much God loved the Irish people by sending them Saint Patrick. We understood how Ireland embraced the gospel and Saint Patrick became the patron saint of Ireland. I recall at night my mother's face so close to mine as we prayed together, "Now I lay me down to sleep, I ask thee Lord my soul to keep. If I should die before I wake, I ask Thee Lord my soul to take." A Catholic prayer we also heard from my mother was "Angel of God, my guardian dear, to whom God's love commits me here. Ever this day be at my side..." my mother was so adept at telling us the most amazing stories but also impressed on us even as small children the sobering realities of the eternal world and the life to come.

We were only at Wiggens Street for a very short while when we realized we had two very special relatives, my mother's sisters, we hadn't met yet. They were nuns and would become the closest relatives to our family in America. They worked at a Catholic orphanage called Mount Loretta in Staten Island, New York. They visited on birthdays, Holy Communions, confirmations, graduations, and other events during the year. When visiting, they stayed at the convent of our local parish at Saint Joseph's Church.

When they came to visit, which was quite often, they brought bags of toys. Their names became synonymous with toys, when we were children, but in time we would grow to love them for the great women they were to our lives. While they were alive, they never missed sending birthday cards with friendly thoughts and blessings. On a number of occasions, we visited the Mount Loretta orphanage as a family. At the time there was no Verrazzano Narrows Bridge and we would take the ferry across to Staten Island. On one occasion while visiting all of us stood outside with them looking up at the high steeple of the church. With the clouds moving across the sky, it appeared as if the steeple was moving. My father perhaps joking made a comment about going up to fix it. As a young boy I believed my father could fix anything. I was mesmerized at the thought of him going way up there to fix a falling steeple that looked to me like Mount Everest. That impression as a small boy lasted throughout my life as I would see my father overcome every difficulty and challenge our family encountered.

On one rare occasion at Wiggens Street we were visited by the oldest sibling of my mother's family, our Uncle Rich. He had emigrated to America before my mother was born. It was a very cordial visit, but we would not see or hear from Uncle Rich again for many years. I do not believe he kept any kind of close relationship or communication with any of the other siblings living in America.

We stayed at this small home in Lake Ronkonkoma for several years and my father faithfully served Mr. Eilerston. As time transpired our family grew larger. Initially it was only myself, my older brother Patrick, and my younger sister Marian. The home had only two bedrooms. My sister Margaret arrived, then my brother Billy and also my brother Joe was on the way. It was becoming very apparent that the home was too small for such a growing family. My father in having kept such a cordial relationship with his boss Mr. Eilerston now contemplated entering the trade he had been training for on the side. He spoke with a gentleman named Frank Muller who owned a drywall business and offered my father a job earning higher pay. Mr. Eilerston was very receptive to my father's decision, and my father accepted Frank Muller's offer.

As the second oldest child I only recall good memories of living on Wiggens Street in Lake Ronkonkoma. In Kindergarten I had a kind teacher whose name was Miss Underwood. It was at that time I remember having my first feelings of self-identity and worth even as a young child. I loved this new country we were in. This special school at Gatelot Avenue in Lake Ronkonkoma represented America to me as something healthy and attractive. Coming home I would look forward to seeing my devoted mother waiting for me at the bus stop. I would share with her about my day as we walked home together. I would enjoy rehearsing songs I learned by singing them to my mother. One morning I remember the bus arriving and I was in the middle of singing a new song to my mother that I had learned in school. The bus had to wait until the song was entirely finished. My mother would share that story even when I became much older. The ability of my mother to have singular moments with each of her children was a defining quality she possessed in raising all of us. I clearly remember how carefully she taught me to ride my first two-wheel bike at the age of five. Both my brother and I had gotten new bikes. Mine had training wheels. The big day arrived when my training wheels came off and my mother would run alongside my bike holding my back saddle. To me I would never have to learn to ride on my own, this is what mothers were supposed to do all the time. I would hear her voice behind me as I peddled along. One day as I was telling her a long story, I did not hear any affirmation, so I swung my head around only to see my mom standing far behind in the middle of the road watching. The bike went straight down in an instant. I cried as if I needed to be peeled from the wreckage. How could she have been so cruel? I recall my mom tenderly putting me back on the bike. In no time I was an expert on my own. Sadly, at that same time my brother Patrick's new bike was stolen.

I distinctly recall going as a family to a large store that sold swing sets and my parents buying us a really beautiful one that was installed for us right after they bought it. Words cannot describe the joy of a child's first swing set. Our old neighbors the Loughlins from Cedar Street in Centereach would visit. They had two very fat daughters, Bettyanne and Arleen. In coming down the slide one day the bottom gave out and was crushed. My brother and I took that episode very badly. One day Bettyanne had a helium balloon on a string that got away. We somberly watched until it was so far away that it vanished from sight. For several years my brother and I would ask each other the question at different times, "I wonder where Bettyanne's balloon is now?" This became a joke that went on much later in life.

One could not communicate how much our loving mother and indefatigable father who worked so hard to provide for his family would make our primitive life at Wiggens St. such a trove of beautiful memories. Every birthday was celebrated and made such an event that as children we yearned for our birthdays to come. Children from the neighborhood were invited and even those from the area where we used to live in Centereach. Every tooth lost in early childhood meant we were to be visited by a fairy at night who would leave a dime under our pillow. Life was always intriguing when you have a strong mother whose entire focus is on her children and their well-being.

It was during this time as a young boy in Wiggens Street that we had a little sister Mary who was born after my sister Margaret. She had only lived a few days and died. This was a tragedy that my mother took very poorly and was inconsolable while in the hospital. My father already knew a Mr. Joe Weber as a fellow usher at St. Joseph's R.C. Church who owned the local funeral home in Lake Ronkonkoma. Mary was baptized and received a proper funeral after her death and Mr. Weber would only accept partial payments for her burial as my father was able to pay. Perhaps this was why my father in business years later would allow people in hardship to send payments as they could afford.

Over the decades all spackling done at Weber's funeral home was performed by our family business. My father, unable to console my mother at that time, was able to solicit help from a priest of our parish, a Father Nasser. He shared with my mother the necessity of her becoming well, that she had children who needed and depended on her at home. With the words that he spoke, my mother recovered, and so did her buoyancy. How much I revered the Church and its outreach to our family. I can remember as a young boy, my mother would recount that story to me. It would impress on me our great need in life to be part of the Church. Emotionally my father would have handled that event much better, but in his very later years he shared with me the heartbreak of holding her little coffin as she was about to be buried. He was the only one there without friends or family. My father possessed that ability to compartmentalize painful situations and not allow emotions to rule even during those times of trauma and deep sorrow. His pain though well managed would linger within his heart for the rest of his life. My mother once commented to me that only once in all the years of their marriage that my father had lost that ability. I share this personal story to convey the love my father had towards his family even though it was often not communicated.

Over 35 years ago my wife and I decided to move to Ireland with our children. My father was very upset with our decision and communicated his displeasure to my mother. In the middle of his conversation, he began weeping. My mother had never encountered such a moment with him. She shared it with me to communicate the deep sorrow my father had about me leaving. We were very engaged together in running our family business and he did not want me to move away.

With the death of my sister Mary, my parents would hold in the highest regard our Roman Catholic faith. With the support of a devout priest and his ministry, my parents were comforted in their time of despair. Another priest would stop by every week with a box of food while we lived at Wiggens Street. This was unsolicited as so many people knew my father and I guess we looked somewhat in need. My father was an usher at that time and was also over The Legion of Mary ministry at St. Joseph's. We would often say the rosary together as a family. All through our years growing up to adulthood, Mass was never missed, nor Holy Days of Obligation, and the Sacraments.

On a particular Sunday during the Christmas season, I asked my mother to bring me forward to see Bethlehem Village that was beautifully rendered by women from the church. It was a difficult request to have made to my mother after Mass, as there were so many smaller children that she was attending to. I remember asking her ever so quietly. Somehow, she intuitively discerned it as a special moment for me and was able to leave the children behind and take my hand to walk forward. I may have been only five or six at the time. I remember standing there quietly mesmerized by the quaint little village of Bethlehem and the stable where Jesus lay. I knew he was born to take away the sins of the world, even mine. It was one of those moments of transfer as we quietly stood looking together at the picturesque village of Bethlehem. My mother's God became my God and I knew He was true and there was no other, and that this truth was in Jesus. I somehow in reminiscing that event sadly never shared it with my mother when she was alive. We were so close and years later my mother paid for a five-star trip for just her and I to go to Israel where we saw the real Bethlehem. That would have been a good place to share this story with her. My mother was very desirous of all of her children embracing the faith that so many Irish of her generation were devoted to following.

At Wiggins Street we were in America for less than one year and were adjusting to a very different culture. I remember our first Halloween. Our home being visited by ghouls. As kids we didn't understand. Perhaps because my mother did not put candy out, we all hid in the back bedroom. I remember being terrified. This holiday actually traces back to Ireland and its Celtic roots, and as children we were not aware of what was happening to us. I had wished my mother would have explained and pacified our fears. It wouldn't be till a later time I would understand our misplaced fears on that night.

As little children we would sit outside our front stoop with our mother at night. We would see the search light from the local airport that would menacingly stream across the sky. We were all convinced about it being a new weapon system the Americans were testing. As very young children living in a new country, we had not yet understood the uniqueness of America and how blessed our lives would be as future citizens.

Chapter 13

New York Telephone

As my father was now a skilled drywall mechanic, my mother began encouraging him towards getting a job that would carry benefits and a pension. My mother wanted security for the future.

During a week that he had vacation my father went into New York City, 101 Willoughby St., Brooklyn, to the New York Telephone Company. My father was fortunate enough to meet an Irish American who was the personnel manager. His name was Jim McFarland. Although there were no present openings, my father was encouraged to take a physical exam at the medical department which he easily passed. When my father returned to his office, he was told a menial job was found out in Suffolk County in the town of Commack, not far from Lake Ronkonkoma where we lived. He would be pumping gas into telephone trucks at night.

My father was advised to take the job to get his foot in the door. My father readily accepted this offer and joined the New York Telephone Company on September 9, 1957. He would spend the next 30 years working this job without ever missing a day. In a congratulatory letter received in 1977 for a perfect attendance record of fourteen years, with only one absence in February of 1963, my father was commended for being such an excellent employee. In a scripted statement written at the bottom of this letter, my father wrote in pen "The above statement is not correct. I never missed a day in 30 years. Note: Phil Payne V.P. was new on the job." This note was signed by my father.

As part of my research in writing this book, I have found information like this delightful, amusing and definitely apropos in describing my father. He was proud of his perfect record of attendance. After a short time of pumping gas, my father was quickly transferred to cleaning buildings where eventually he became a night foreman over several buildings. Every year my father was awarded a certificate for maintaining the cleanest buildings in Suffolk County. My father over the years was recommended for higher positions within the company, but would decline because he had a thriving drywall business during the day which far exceeded any salary, he could receive from a day position at the telephone company. After retiring from the phone company at 65 years old, my father continued working actively in drywall until he was 84 years old. Falling off a ladder working at my sister's house, he had hurt his hand and refused therapy. He could no longer hold the tools properly, which brought him into full retirement nearly 20 years after leaving the phone company. For over thirty years of his life my father had worked two full time jobs to provide for his large family. From the time of leaving school as a young boy to help support his family in Ireland my father had worked nearly 75 years. I never heard a complaint from him concerning work or life's challenges.

With the New York Telephone Company as employment, my parents could qualify for a mortgage. A larger home was the next order of business and more room for the children to play. The American dream was now within reach. My father was now gainfully employed by one of the strongest companies in New York. From a young boy my father became intimately acquainted with hard work and now with the offer of working only 80 hours per week, that dream was within reach

Chapter 14

Attending School at St. Joseph's

Around the time of my father starting work at the phone company my brother had started attending parochial school at our local parish. I started the following year and it was perhaps one of the most torturous and damaging years of my life. It would have been naturally understood that starting first grade was going to be an even more surpassing experience than Kindergarten. After all it was where we attended church and were taught about God. A Mrs. Desmond was an abusive first grade teacher waiting to persecute and emotionally damage her young innocent students. As a young child I would struggle with feelings that I was very stupid and had little worth. Only my mother's love mollified the abuse I experienced in the first grade by this teacher. Her class each day resembled that of being in a war camp. In Ireland, during my mother's time, it was accepted that teachers could physically punish and emotionally lambast children with impunity, as it was universally accepted that children needed to be brought into submission. The emotional damage and trauma experienced by the child was little thought about. When I would tell my mother that early on in the school year how row assignments were made that placed students in particular rows that would define their mental abilities and skills or lack thereof. There were six rows that made up fifty students. The first row from the door was called the busy beavers, then there were the squirrels. The sixth row where I sat was called *the dumbbells*. It seemed apparent that the further back you sat on this row, the dumber you were. To this day sixty-four years later I still remember the first and last names of the two boys who sat behind me. The last seat was occupied by a boy who would clearly be understood today as being mentally challenged.

Out of the whole class this teacher had a vendetta for me beyond the other children that I could not understand. As a young boy I would be comforted every day by a mother who I knew loved and affirmed me. I could not understand why each day I would be brutalized in front of the entire class. It was only a matter of time and I began having involuntary physiological responses to her treatment. As she would go up each row of children with questions, my legs would shake uncontrollably as she would get to my row. The other children would call out to Mrs. Desmond, "Kieran's legs are shaking!" "Well, they will be more than shaking when I get to him!" she would respond. I would always hope that the question would be one I could answer. Invariably that was not what usually happened. It would be a hard question and I would be ridiculed in front of the entire class. I experienced brain freezes that immobilized me. On a particular day I was taken in front of the class and lambasted severely as I stood dumbfounded in front of simple equations. Mrs. Desmond contemptuously grilled me in front of the class with anger and ridicule over my inability to answer her question.

One day while she was doing this I began praying and asking God to help me, I kept telling Him that I could not think and would He please help me? Perhaps my earliest memory of Divine intervention in life was that in the middle of my prayer as Mrs. Desmond was assailing me, I felt as if something smooth poured into my brain and all mental confusion left. I immediately understood every equation and began going straight down the line across the entire blackboard answering every equation. As I went across the blackboard, I remember becoming exhilarated with confidence. I had a "know" infused into my being that I never experienced before. By the time I finished the last equation, I confidently placed the chalk on the small rail under the blackboard. At the same time her hand hit my head so hard that it bounced off the blackboard and she said, "Why didn't you do that in the first place?"

What happened with my head hitting the backboard was painless I recall, but I left school that day as a changed person. Nobody would ever understand what had just happened but my mother would. I couldn't wait to get home to tell her. When I arrived home my mother was cleaning the kitchen. The table was still wet and I began doing equations on the wet table with my finger. I was so excited as I wrote out different equations. With new mental ability, I now felt empowered. My mother very upset shared information she had received that questioned Mrs. Desmond's credentials and lack of education qualifying her to be a teacher.

During my next episode with Mrs. Desmond, I was again singled out in front of the class but this time I began reciting in front of the class everything I heard my mother say about her being an unqualified teacher. I had a strength and courage visit me that I couldn't understand. Mrs. Desmond's timidness at first during my declaration had even surprised me, but then she stretched forth her hand and politely asked me to stop, which I did. She had ordered the class to leave the room and wait outside. She sat at her desk and said, "Now Kieran, tell me everything your mother said about me." As a young boy only six years old, I was more than willing to share with her all the deficits my mother had spoken to me about her. As she wrote she held an angry grimace with her tongue protruding out of the side of her mouth. Her pen moved furiously on the page. It was an event somehow indelibly placed upon my mind. When I arrived home and placed the letter into my mother's hand, she began reading. I saw my mother's eyes get larger as she read the letter. My mother's lips were moving as if she were sounding out each word in the letter. Finally, she looked at me upset and said, "What did you say to her?" I told my mother the truth that I repeated to the teacher what I heard her say.

My mother being upset still stood her ground and comforted me. Somehow after that event Mrs. Desmond never bothered me again. She would place other unfortunate children before the class with a dunce hat, on a chair, but I never recall her singling me out again. A small boy needing to go to the bathroom badly and cringing in his chair as he held his hand over himself in order not to wet his pants was yelled at to get out and go to the *lavatory*. While away from the class Mrs. Desmond instructed the children that upon his return everyone would stand and point at him scolding with one index finger over the other and speak a rhyme, "Shame, shame, baby shame, you wet your pants..." When the boy returned, he made it as far as the door, and the class arose and repeated Mrs. Desmond's words. The boy let out a heartbreaking cry and ran out of the room. We never saw him back in class again. It wouldn't be until the end of the year that I found out that I was left back. Her malice would not be assuaged. It was a vendetta she would hold on to.

On the last day of school my brother met me outside the school bus in the school parking lot. I told him I was left back. So was he in the second grade. He warned me straightly to not let Jimmy Bruno know if he should ask. We were no sooner on the bus and the question was asked by none other than Jimmy Bruno. I told him that I was left back and so also was my brother Patrick. This resulted in the whole bus chanting all the way to our home, "Left back Mac!, left back Mac!" It was a comfort to know getting off the bus that day that a horrible year had passed and that summer was now just beginning and school would not have to be thought about till September. The whole year had been a living a nightmare. The thought of repeating such a year hurt me significantly as a young boy. But through the trauma, I had an experience with God, that was undeniable. He had rescued me from deep waters of affliction and pain, at the hands of a ruthless person. My mother's comfort and encouragement gave me a strong sense of security. It would be the first Divine intervention I experienced during my life, and thankfully many would follow as I got older.

Someday this could become a future book by itself. My mother's God was the true God who watched over us and who was willing to intervene at crucial times. And as for the terrible bully we would endure for years, my brother kept growing and Jimmy would look smaller every year. Patrick became a fearless fighter. Perhaps the worst I've ever seen anyone get beat up was years later as Jimmy was roughing me up, and my brother jumped out of some bushes. My brother had an Irish gene that never visited me, that for centuries gave Ireland the proud tradition of producing champion fighters.

As that summer ended, I would be reminded daily that something horrible awaited me around the corner in school. The day finally came that I was to go with my mother and meet my new first grade teacher. It was going to be a nun this time and they were even more frightening than lay teachers. How would I ever go through such a trial again? When my mother and I stood together with this nun, my mother quietly shared about my difficult experience with Mrs. Desmond. She placed her hand on my face and spoke God's blessing and very kind words. It would become a very good year and I would flourish through the rest of grammar school, high school and college. I would eventually after graduating from college oversee a cost-accounting area in a large corporation producing in excess of several hundred million dollars per year. In my early thirties however, I returned to our family drywall business to see my income immediately double through my father's generosity. We would never have a bad or a slow year even during recessions. My education and accounting background helped me run a very successful drywall business throughout Long Island.

My parents did their best to provide an education for all their children that would also provide the knowledge of God. The best churches, institutions and even families are often not exempt from the destructive power of evil and sin. And the best person and most kind engages an everyday battle within their own hearts to be free from that which only the grace of God can remove. Because this internal struggle lies intrinsically within every person, we are therefore to forgive, as we also need mercy and forgiveness. As I have observed the parenting skills of my own children, I have often reflected how much better a father I could have been myself. It would almost be providential that years later Mrs. Desmond was a customer on my paper route. She treated me as if I'd been one of her favorite students. It would heal a deep wound. She would go on to teach fifth grade and be loved by all of her students, including my younger siblings. It might be commented by an older sibling in our family why I left out some of the mistakes and deficits of people in the story of our family, especially my parents.

Although everything written is an accurate account, I have chosen to accentuate the positive experiences of my parents and family. As with Mrs. Desmond, people can and often do change. My mother would feel ignored by my father through much of their marriage. His busy life and involvement with Irish music and culture made her feel sidelined by the person she most loved. In our intimate sharing and conversation, I would tell my mother that someday she would have my father back, and until then she had my sisters and those who surrounded her with love in our large family.

In 1997 my father retired as the North American Chairman of Comhaltias Ceoltoiri Eireann. As the North American founder of this organization, it eventually became the foremost cultural institute of Ireland, to promote and foster traditional Irish music, song, dance and also the Irish language. My father began to travel extensively with my mother to faraway places and they were together more than my mother in earlier years could ever have imagined. There would be three trips to Hawaii, two trips to Alaska, and a river cruise through countries in Europe and areas of Russia. they would enjoy trips to Aruba and Cancun, Mexico with my sisters. As they got even older my father would become redefined as the most attentive and caring husband. As my mother became sick with Parkinson's disease, my father's attentiveness increased even more dramatically. They would still travel and go places, especially the local branch on Long Island for Irish music and dancing in Mineola. My father also became more involved in the lives of his children and even some of his many grandchildren.

Delays are often not denials. That which had been despaired of by my praying mother would visit her later in life to become a renaissance of joy and satisfaction. People as my parents, and especially my father, enter new seasons of life. My father in his later years became completely the man my mother had longed and waited for to return. His conversations with me became very personal and engaging, whereas before it was always about business. In his later years my father became my best friend. After my mother's death he would tell me stories of his life and Ireland and share regrets over things he would like to have done better, especially for my mother. He would ask me always about an estranged son who hadn't spoken to him in many years. He would be sorry and disheartened by a grandson that did not communicate with any member of our family. He would travel to Florida to see that grandson who had many wounds and emotional hurts. My father had a desire to mollify those hurts in any way he could.

Our parents are often the people most needed to help us succeed and overcome life and many of its brutal challenges. Each parent often provides that different place of need in our lives. I loved my dad's energy, and throughout my life I would be the same. He was never cornered by life. My mother exhibited that love and nurturing spirit that still visits my life with tears. We never outgrow that need for love, acceptance and affirmation. She would call me *Keeney*, my pet name, even on her death bed, before she left this world.

Wiggens Street was a chapter in our lives that as the second oldest of our large family, was full of memories that I will always treasure. A bond developed between my mother and I that would last until my early sixties when she breathed her last.

Chapter 15

Our New Home in Lake Grove

The time had arrived for the next move, to leave our beloved home with its small yard and look for something bigger to meet the needs of a growing family. As with Wiggins Street it would require the same Providential reach and blessing that my parents had experienced throughout their lives.

I remember that exciting time for my parents when they began looking for that next home. We had been looking at homes in areas around Lake Ronkonkoma where we presently lived. They were larger homes on residential streets. Somehow my parents were waiting for that special home, and then it happened. One town north of Lake Ronkonkoma was a town called Lake Grove. An older couple, the Overtons were selling a small farm of just under three acres with a two-story house and three barns. They planned to move in with their daughter and her family next door. It was located on a main street with a fair amount of traffic that would pass each day. The price of the home was within the budget of my parents at the time.

I remember my parents going out to look at the house and my father putting me up on his shoulders as we took a walk around the property. It was a wonderland for children. There were still chickens running around. There was such amicable conversation between my father and the aged Mr. Overton on that day. As a young boy only six years old I knew something special was happening. My mother loved the home. Her dream was to own such a home. With adjoining fields everywhere, it was far more rural than Lake Ronkonkoma. It didn't take long to decide. My father shook hands with Mr. Overton. As children we could not have been more excited, especially my older brother and I.

My parents' mortgage was approved quickly by the nearby Tinker National Bank. Our family was moving to a new home beyond our imaginations. It was 1958, our fourth year in America. My father had undertaken small construction projects in the home before we had moved in. I went from sharing a small bedroom with many noisy siblings to having my own bedroom. The weather was warm when we moved in and my older brother and I were burning with adventure. To go from a tiny home on a small parcel of land in Lake Ronkonkoma to owning a larger home on nearly three acres was nearly inconceivable to our family. To us children, the barns were the best part of the story. There were two chicken coups and one large barn with a hayloft on top. The hayloft was still full of hay. Our friends, Ralph and Harry Swanson who lived one street over from us in Lake Ronkonkoma would come over every weekend. We would explore every part of the property including the old farmhouse. A closet adjoining the kitchen had a trap door that led to a very dingy old basement. We were convinced a very old woman was kept down there away from our family so she could not harm anyone.

This was at a time in America especially rural areas where children were safe to be outside and alone all day long. My mother was now living the dream that she held from the time of a small girl in Ireland. She was busy with younger children, but she knew that all of her children would have plenty of room to play as they got older.

We quickly became friends with the family next door, the Halberstadts. The wife's name was Beulah and her husband was Dick, a Suffolk County police officer. They had two children, Donna and Kevin. The Overton's lived there also who were the parents of Beulah. The second house further south on the same side of the street was the Furmans, Milt and Evelyn who had two adopted sons, Johnny and Dave. Dave became one of my closest friends.

The Adventures of Huckleberry Finn would have been a good way to describe the kind of life we had living on what was formerly a farm. Large open areas surrounded our property with substantial woods filled with all kinds of trees. Next to one of the chicken coups was a tall tree that my brother bravely climbed with a rope to tie on a large branch. We jumped from the flat roof of the chicken coup out into thin air for the most exhilarating ride that would make us feel like a bird flying. A game was invented that we called Coutie. One person would be on the top of the flat sloping barn roof.

All the other children would make every attempt to get on top of the roof. The person on the roof would step on the fingers of the person trying to get on top and yell, "Coutie!" While stepping on the fingers of a person on one side of the barn, another kid would be climbing up the other side, and perhaps get on top which would make him the new *King* who was ready to stomp on the next coutie trying to get on top. We would play this game for hours at a time. My mother could be seen out at the clothes line looking across contentedly at her children playing.

As young boys it was only just a matter of time and we became explorers. The neighboring fields and woods had intrigued us for so long. As we would travel into these uncharted areas, it was the greatest time of excitement we had experienced thus far in our short lives. We became enchanted with discovering what lay beyond the areas surrounding our small farm.

Only a handful of years earlier my mother fell in love with a man from County Laois while walking home from a dancehall in County Kerry where they walked along together under the largest brightest full moon. To give my mother and the children this life would come at a price. My father worked two full time jobs over the course of many decades without complaint. Despite all the years of hard work my father would comment to me before his death about "How hard your mammy had it." My father's Darwinian concept of life and working so hard to survive never gave way to grumbling or complaint. Both parents were tempered from early childhood to not only survive but thrive in difficult circumstances.

One day as a young boy I was intrigued by my father making something that he was very focused on completing. It was a "V" shaped sign that could be seen on our busy road from both directions of traffic. I watched my father when he was carefully finished painting with a small brush using black paint his name, Bill McEvoy *Spackling and Taping* and our phone number the third line down. This was a momentous decision that resulted in securing a substantial business for the remainder of his life. The home my parents bought fortunately was located on a main road with a lot of traffic. That traffic would substantially increase as a large expressway called the Long Island Expressway finally reached Hawkins Avenue where we lived. This highway when complete became one of the busiest roads in the state of New York stretching from New York City across most of Long Island. At that time within a couple of miles of my parents' address one of the largest malls on Long Island was also being built. The street we lived on was a main street connecting Smith Haven Mall to the Long Island Expressway. Traffic substantially increased on our road and my father's business grew correspondingly.

My father's sign predated the incorporation of the village of Lake Grove and all attempts to remove the sign by the village in court were rebuffed. My father as a result would constantly be supplied an inexhaustible amount of work. The prosperity of our entire family was changed permanently when they chose this location as their new home. Purchasing this residence shortly before Lake Grove became an incorporated village could not have been calculated better. This properly seen was another example of Providence reaching through to my father's life and providing a business that probably otherwise would not have existed. My father continued working for Frank Muller for just a short while longer after the sign went up, and then launched entirely into his own drywall business and began hiring men. My father stayed connected to Frank Muller as friends for many years, and often referenced how honorable a businessman he was while working for him. My father would stay with the phone company for nearly 30 years while conducting his own business. Through his mid-sixties he continued working both jobs full time. After retiring from the phone company at the age of sixty-six, he would remain doing drywall until he was 84.

In true Irish form my father would say how much my mother would get by on so little, but being the only son closely involved in this business, my father was a great provider and no-one ever lacked. Both he and my mother were incapable of saying no to any of their children, even to their later years. My mother was a very frugal person in handling money and always carefully saved for a rainy day.

And when as a family we were all finally well situated, my father turned his focus to that appointment with destiny and calling on his life of becoming a conduit of what he loved to do the most. He would promote Irish culture, music and dance and bring it to an entire hemisphere.

Chapter 16

Father's Early Days in Ireland

It was in the late 1950's that my father's eyes began turning back to his native country. He made the first of around one hundred thirty-eight trips to Ireland that took place every year for the remainder of his life. In the course of time, he would travel several times a year to see his family, friends and more specifically to become involved with Irish music and culture events. This was the beginning of when transatlantic flights became the standard means of travel by everyone who would now rather fly than travel by boat. My father traversed everywhere throughout Ireland where these special festivals and events called Ceilis, and fleadh's were taking place. As a young boy my father worked on a large Protestant farm that enabled him with his mother's permission to buy a new bicycle. This bicycle enabled him to travel throughout his area and even to other nearby counties to attend these events and music sessions.

For centuries this was celebrated all over the country in every county. They attracted well known musicians, step dancers and performing artists from every part of Ireland. Music was provided by talented harpist, accordionist, flute, tin whistle, uillean pipe players and great fiddlers, guitar and banjo. Accomplished step dancers including traditional set dancing were always part of every festival. The musicians played jigs and reels and accompanied those who sang ballads of Ireland's history and political oppression. Songs of love and pathos about emigration, and leaving Ireland were common themes. Long before *Woodstock* ever happened the Irish were celebrating music and their distinctive culture that was far more pure and less prurient than what is contemporarily celebrated by many today. Here my father would meet people and become very acquainted with notable performers and great musicians. This became the archetype for building an umbrella of traditional Irish music for North America. He would in future help build an organization that identified Irish music and culture in its purest form, and place chapters in areas where Irish people lived throughout the United States and parts of Canada.

My father was perhaps the most loyal person I've ever known to his friends. Every trip to Ireland involved stops at the homes of friends in every county throughout Ireland. Although my father could spend all of this time visiting notable people, most visits were with primitive and obscure lovers of Ireland as himself who shared a common passion and background. Many were the boyhood friends that played hurling with him or family members that were practically beyond count. He would visit his parents with cognizance always of their financial needs. My father being the oldest of six children would visit each of his younger siblings except his sister Molly who lived in England. His loyalty caused him to visit the graves of those he loved as a young boy. I stood with him one day in the graveyard outside his boyhood church in Knockaroo, County Laois as he shared with me the stories of some of these people. A Mrs. Nora Campion was a teacher of special boyhood endearment and so many other friends who were born, lived and died in that area of Knockaroo, County Laois where he also attended school.

My father as an avid fan of hurling, would personally know the stories of the great athletes of his boyhood days and share the memory of these giants of his time. One was a friend Tommy Fitzpatrick, a star player in hurling. My father often talked about an All-Ireland game that was played in 1915 when his county won the national championship. Born in 1923 my father knew many of these great players as he got older. At the age of 10 my father attended his first All-Ireland hurling final with his father in Dublin.

These trips to Ireland allowed my father to endure the frenetic lifestyle of work and very little sleep. His indomitable wife would raise his children, and his indefatigable strength would make sure all the bills were paid. All of his children would lack for nothing.

When I was twelve years old in 1964, my parents decided to go back and visit Ireland as a family. This was one of the most exciting events of my life up to that point. The homeland of my parent's, and the place of my birth. We visited aunts and uncles and cousins on both my mother and father's side. My father's parents were still alive. It was very memorable. We stayed a lot of time in Kerry at Banemore where I was born. My uncle Mick, my mother's brother was my favorite, and would give me my own horse to ride and explore all over Banemore. I would contemplate my mother's own younger years as a young girl growing up here and all the adventures, she had communicated to us as children. On one occasion my parents were out with friends and family. Uncle Mick watched us for the night, and we slept in the same room where I was born. He was such a congenial man who could tell incredible stories even surpassing those of my mother. The house had no bathroom and when I would step outside to go, I'd be so frightened in the pitch-black night. Was there a Banshee waiting with her long hair and a comb, I wondered? Uncle Micks' stories were so frightening and I was very much a glutton for punishment. His gentle voice and kindly manner augmented his storytelling.

While visiting Kerry we would do the famous Ring of Kerry that could compare with beauty to be found anywhere on planet earth. My mother would contrast my father's county with her own in a display of one-upmanship and rivalry. This bantering would extend into other areas like sports and the famed County Kerry All Ireland champion footballers. My father however was a great Kerry lover and rooted for them throughout his life.

Our large family was crowded into a large station wagon. My older brother and I sat on the open back tailgate of the car with our feet almost touching the road as we drove along. Had we fallen off, my father would never have known. On one of these small scenic roads, we passed a cyclist and in perhaps one of the most brazen acts of American punkery, sass and insolence, my brother spit at a cyclist hitting him square. The spurned cyclist shifted his bike into high gear and pursued after us as my father unwittingly meandered smoothly along in clueless serendipity. This was a lad who looked like he was about to do damage. He got so close that we could see the veins bulging on his neck. When he reached the car, I was sure he would let the bike go and jump in on us like a leopard and tear us to pieces. My brother let out a plaintive cry to my father, "Dad, speed up, go faster!" Fortunately, we came to a steep climb and soon the cyclist was far out of sight. My mother and father were both unaware. Had my father known, he would probably have been a worse choice than meeting the enraged cyclist. I was just hoping that there were no upcoming souvenir shops to be seen or bathroom stops needed for the rest of that day.

In County Laois where my father was from, we again met so many family members. My father being the oldest had a special relationship with all his siblings. The friendship of our family to our Irish relatives was something we never experienced before. This was our identity and background. It was who we really were, connected to our real family and friends. Everywhere we went were first cousins, aunts and uncles. One day I walked with my father to a beautiful outside spring where I imagine he fetched water as a boy. I had never up to that point in life seen my father in a happier disposition. What was it about Ireland that had such an effect on the person of my father? Perhaps in the history of Ireland and all of its stories of emigration, very few would match my father's story of loyalty and love in traveling back so many times through his mid-nineties.

The endearment of my father to his parents was understood by me even as a young boy, especially to his mother. Several days before we were to head back to America, my father's mother began weeping for her Willie. Perhaps now is a good time to share a story about my father mentioned earlier in this writing that I had not yet expounded on. In my father's late eighties, it was decided that I would accompany him on his trips to Ireland. Advanced arthritis began to affect his ability to walk and drive. I looked forward to these trips as I knew it brought real happiness to him and it was also a time to hear new stories not heard before. As a younger man neither my older brother nor myself had much of a conversational relationship with my father. When my sister Marian died and then my mother several months later, something changed and my father and I became very close. He was then nearly ninety-four years old.

On a particular night while having dinner with my father at an airport restaurant, he shared with me how as a young boy he would see his mother crying. She was a devout Catholic woman who my father said was always praying. My father knew as a young boy that the family was in financial trouble, even to the point of losing their small farm in County Laois. My father as a person with a call of destiny on his life loved education and school. At or around the age of ten, he made the decision to leave school and go up the road to work at a large Protestant farm and give all of his pay to his mother to help keep their own farm and pay expenses. Although my father's father was a man of excellent character and sweet temperament, years of being incarcerated, mistreated, and starved as an IRA soldier and prisoner of war, by the English had perhaps affected his ability to run their small farm. My father as a young boy had a high level of perception and discernment towards this. He knew the family needed help and his responsibility as the oldest required him to embrace what hardly anyone his age would ever do. He went to his mother and shared his plan of working on the Protestant farm to help pay expenses. My father shared that on the day he spoke to his mother that she looked at him in a way that he had never seen before. When he was finished, she spoke words over him with tears in her eyes. She said that he would prosper in his life at everything he put his hands to, and that he would live a long life in health.

Even as a young boy the event imprinted itself upon my father and stayed in his memory for the rest of his life. He knew he had stepped into something. When my father had shared that event with me, it was like a curtain was pulled back and I understood something that had always intrigued me from the time I was a young boy. It was something I prayed about as I got older, as it was something paradoxical that I could not understand. My father was not devout in his belief system as one who showed any spiritual fervor as my mother. Yet he walked through life as one that had great favor on all his affairs. As he shared that story, I finally understood something about God as if a secret that had just been revealed to me.

When I was a boy, I used to enjoy watching the Twilight Zone with Rod Serling. Invariably it was about someone stepping into some tale of the supernatural and surreal that seemed inexplicable. Actually, I personally believe that my father as a young boy stepped into a *blessing* that was irrevocably placed upon his life by God. In the ancient Greek there were two words used to describe time. One was called chronos where we get the word chronological or sequential time. The other word is called Kairos that is more qualitative. It means the right or opportune time, a moment of grace and spiritual opportunity. Behind the scenes of an ordinary day, desperation and courage collided. A choice was made that catapulted my father into Divine destiny that placed God's scepter upon the words of my grandmother. The words his mother spoke over him resonated in heaven and God placed a mantle of favor on his life to fulfill everything that was said. He exemplified selfless behavior in rising to the challenge as the oldest of all the siblings, even though he was still a boy. At such a young age his temperament to perform and to be a future leader was becoming apparent. Years later after he left the farm, he placed a good job in Dublin with the

Great Northern Railroad. He met strategic key people connected to his job, and also while in Dublin made association with the pioneers of what would one day become the foremost cultural institute of Ireland, of which he would become the North American founder. Working in Dublin he continued to satisfy his parents debts with local businesses and the supply stores they purchased from. My father never once had a disparaging word about his father but revered and loved his father till his death. When both he and his father went to his first All -Ireland hurling match in Dublin as a young boy, it started a lifelong devotion to Irish sports which was surpassed only by his love of music.

As this book was started and I would spend those treasured moments of inquiry with my father, he shared with me that his father was often complimented by neighbors which resulted in him leaving their home and going off to work for a couple of days on someone else's house. This caused important tasks on their own home not to be accomplished. My father was disturbed by this even at an early age knowing the needs of their own family were more requisite, and that his father was being manipulated by flattery. As the most generous person I have ever known, my father knew how to help people. My father however was the greatest provider to his own family first. We never knew what it meant to lack anything necessary for a happy life. My parents were there to help us through every difficulty and financial need even long years after we were married and left home. Their indefatigable strength throughout their lives and love for all their children would cause them to help out in every need even while paying for the constant two full time aides required to take care of them.

As my father went through life at every juncture or place of difficulty, there were constant interventions that overruled difficult situations and my father would come out on top. His mother always looked upon her son with deep love, never forgetting his willingness to sacrifice his future for the family. My father went on to be self-educated and among other things would write articles in Irish publications on music and culture read by Irish everywhere. He could extemporaneously recite long poems and prose from Irish authors and poets and song writers. In trips to Ireland, we would sometimes visit notable locations like Avoca, County Wicklow where the great Irish poet Thomas Moore penned his famous Irish melody at The Meeting of the Waters where the Avonmore and Beg rivers magically come together to form the Avoca River. One day as we stood before this beautiful scene, my father sang from the lyrics that he knew by heart since he was a boy.

"There is not in this wide world a valley so sweet
As that vale in whose bosom the bright waters meet!
Oh, the last rays of feeling and life must depart
Ere the bloom of that valley shall fade from my heart"

As my father sang through all the lyrics our eyes welled up with tears not just for the beautiful poetic words of Thomas Moore but my father's plaintive voice and his love for the rich culture of Ireland.

On our last trip to Ireland in 2019 before Covid-19 when my father was ninety-six, my two sisters Colleen and Kathleen and myself accompanied my father and visited so many places of resonant memory that echoed stories from his past and also that of my mother. While in Kerry, we stayed at the beautiful Listowel Arms Hotel in the tourist town of Listowel where my sister Marian was baptized. We secured a large conference room overlooking a scenic area and invited our friends and relatives from the area. In times past my father would stop at the homes of people to visit but now that was becoming more difficult as he was infirmed by arthritis. My father was able to eloquently share his love and fond memories of Ireland and its people to a large room of family and friends. After around forty minutes I quite wondered how such a trove of memories and stories could be shared impromptu and unrehearsed. His lack of formal education had not defined his life nor the life of his beautiful bride whose education was also thwarted by life's circumstance and many challenges. He repeated his rhetorical performance of storytelling at the Killeshan Hotel in Port Laois next to the home of Ann Whelan our first cousin, where much of his family and friends from County Laois were also invited. He loved all of his family in County Laois. Over sixty years of visits to Ireland transpired from that first flight back in 1958. It would create a legacy remembered by all of our family and our connectedness to the country both my parents loved so dearly.

That trip to Ireland in 1964 was one of the rare events that our entire family enjoyed together. Our family around that time reached nine children. After returning from Ireland the subject of home expansion was regularly mentioned. Eventually my parents decided it was time for this event to happen, and my father now having many builders that he worked for, contracted for one to double the size of the house by putting a downstairs and upstairs addition onto the house with an attached two car garage. This project went forward and in no time the house was finished and very expanded. The front living room doubled in size with a beautiful stone fireplace also being added. There was now a large home on a large piece of property in the village of Lake Grove, a very safe place to live. My father during the time of his children getting older with their increasing requisite financial needs worked incessantly. My mother would not allow us to be unreflective of his sacrifice. And my mother was just as dutiful towards the wellbeing of her family.

Dad with Kieran and Pat in Ireland

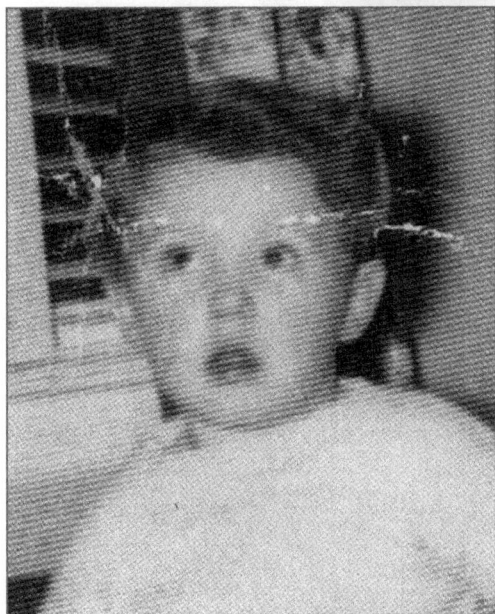

Kieran as a baby

Mom at Banemore with Kieran and Pat

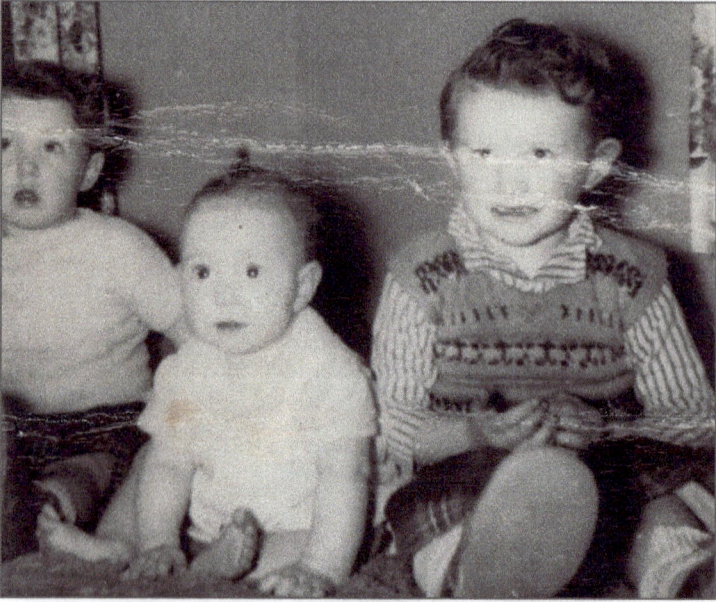

An early picture of Kieran, Pat and Marian

Mom at Wiggens Street with the oldest four children

Kieran's birthday party

Pat's birthday party

Kieran

Track car days

Dad playing his fiddle in early travels back to Ireland

Mom and Aunt Eileen with nuns

Our oldest sister Marian on her wedding day

Our nine children: Patrick, Kieran, Marian, Margaret, Joseph, Lillian, Billy, Colleen and Kathleen

ʒo raibh tú daibhir i mí-áidh	May you be poor in misfortune,
aʒus saibhir i mbeannachtaí	Rich in blessings,
ʒo mall aʒ déanamh namhaid,	Slow to make enemies,
ʒo luath a déanamh carad,	quick to make friends,
ach saibhir nó daibhir,	But rich or poor, quick or slow,
ʒo mall nó ʒo luath,	May you know nothing but happiness
nach raibh ach áthas aʒat	From this day forward.
Ón lá seo amach.	

Early family photo

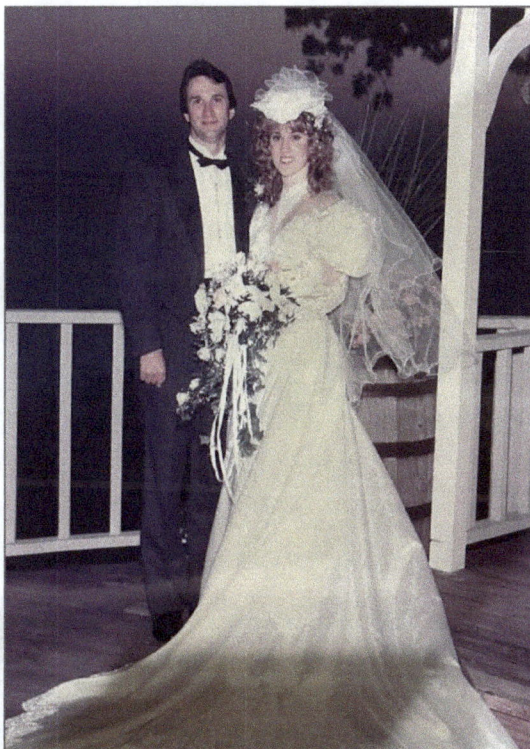

Our youngest sister Kathleen and Jim on their wedding day

Family picture 1990

Christmas 2011

SPECIAL MOMENTS REMEMBERED
AS WE START A NEW YEAR

This year we welcomed our third great grandchild; Connor McEvoy

Great grandchildren Liam & Evan continue to fill our lives with joy and laughter

On 7/1, our granddaughter Siobhan wed Anthony Casimano in Florence, Italy

Dad with his fiddle

Our sister Lillian and George on their wedding day

Dad playing fiddle with the "Bob Morris Band"

Mom and Colleen

Dad at an event

Gerry and Mom dancing at our son Sean's wedding

Mom and Dad with Labhras and Irish Ministers

Dad and Marian

*Family photos at our sister
Colleen and Bob's wedding*

Family photo

Mom and Dad

Mom with great-granddaughters

Mom with Marian and Colleen

Mom and Colleen

Family photo

Dad, Kieran and his son Kevin at an NYC museum

County Laois,
Ireland
Association
honoring
Dad with a
plaque

Dad with great-
grandson Liam

Dad at his birthday
celebration

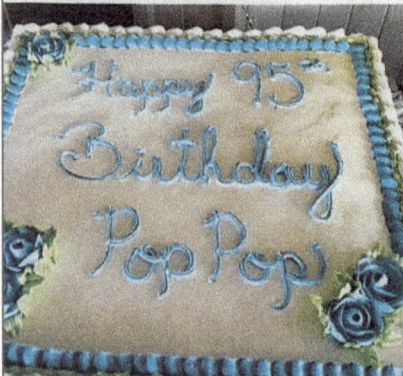

Dad's 95th birthday pictures

Merry Christmas

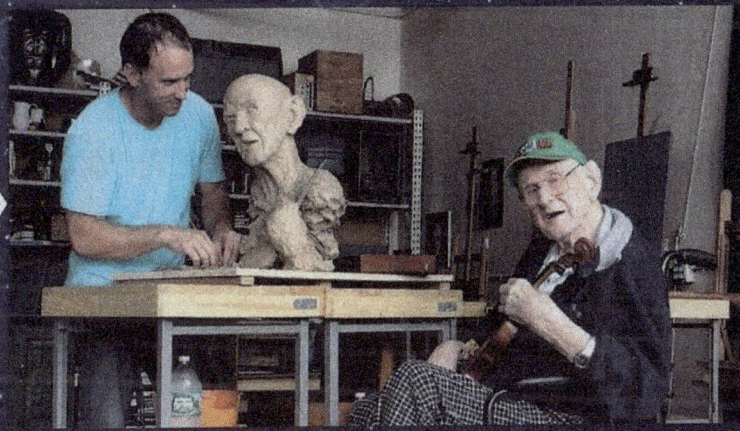

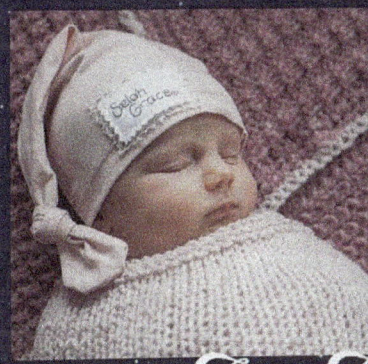

From The McEvoy Family

Evan, Dad and Quin

Dad and Labhras

Dad being honored posthumously in Dublin, Ireland

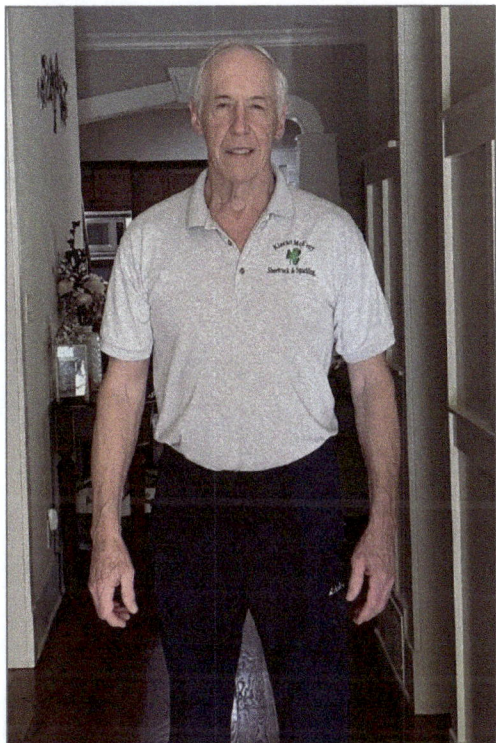

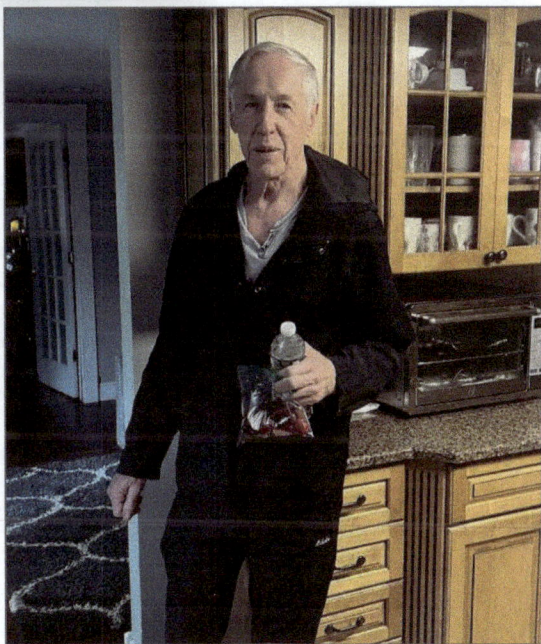

Kieran at home in Collierville, Tennessee

Kieran's son Kevin and his family

Kieran's grandsons sailing

Gerry with grand-daughters Mara and Avery

Kieran's daughter Colleen

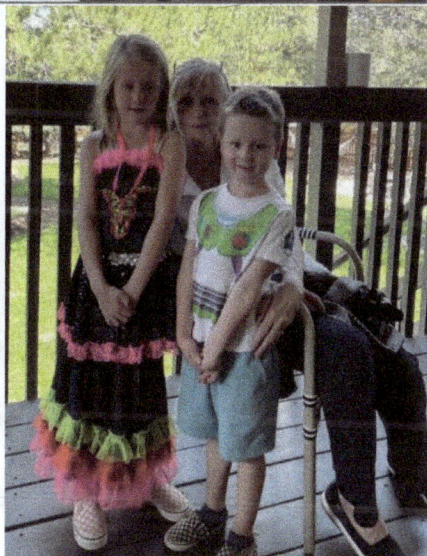

Gerry with grandchildren Adalynn and Declan

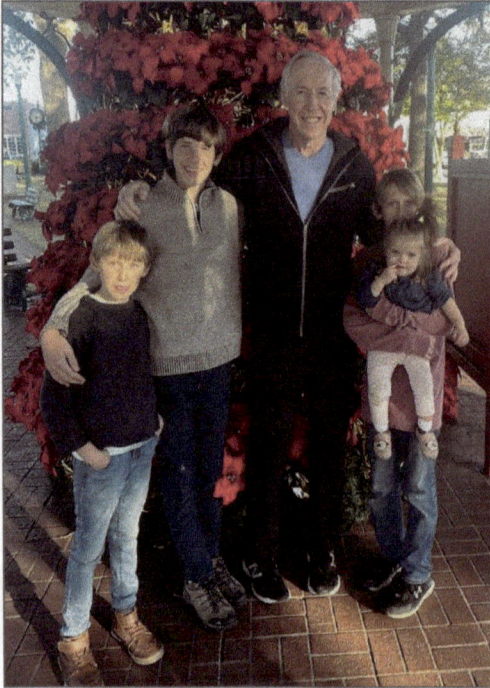

*Kieran with grandchildren
Liam, Evan, Quinlin, and
Fiona*

*Kieran's oldest son Sean
and Justina with their
children*

Kieran's youngest son Christian and Meghan with their children Adalynn and Declan

Kieran's family picture

Dad admiring a sculpture of himself

Chapter 17

Life in Lake Grove

One of the privileges of writing this narrative about our Irish family is I get the liberty to write this story from my perspective and share some events that affected me personally. This imprimatur was granted to me personally by my father in his commission with the appeal that I would simply get the job done. My sisters seemed to have a place of endearment with my father that we as sons did not possess when we were children. My sister Marian waited each day in vigil for my father to come home. When his truck would pull up the driveway wherever she was, she would immediately stop whatever she was doing and run outside before my father ever got out of his truck, delightfully screaming "Daddy doodie! Daddy doodie! Daddy doodie!" Marian through all of her life was love personified especially to my father.

As a boy I would throw our round bouncy ball over to my father as he walked from his truck to our house and with one kick, he would send it over the tops of the trees. No matter how hard I would attempt for years to replicate my father's technique I could not accomplish the blow of his one kick. And he would do that one kick without breaking stride as he walked toward the front door of the house. My father had a dinner waiting for him, he would make some business calls and then eventually head to bed to get just a few hours sleep, and then leave for his second full time job with the phone company. Often, he would stay awake and watch The Jack Benny Show or The Honeymooners. My father had the heartiest laugh when watching these shows. As a young boy I would have the most tranquil feeling hearing my father laughing as I knew he worked so hard. My father would also love to be served, as all of us, my mother's Irish soda bread, and her special soda bread made with currents (or raisins). She had a special recipe handed down to her from her mother and her mother's mother before her. Years later she would always send me home with enough for my own whole family to enjoy.

During the summer sometimes we'd go to Fire Island which faces the Atlantic Ocean. Running parallel against Long Island it boasts to be among one the finest places in the world for white sand beaches. It was always interesting to watch my father in the water at the ocean, as often there would be large waves crashing on the shore. My father would stand and place his shoulder against the crashing waves which would hit him like the Rock of Gibraltar. As the waves hit him relentlessly ejecting spray off his body, he would turn to the gazing spectators of his family with roaring laughter. My father had no ability to swim as most Irish people we knew. On a particular occasion my brother and I had a race on the beach with my father. Somehow, I thought this would be an event in which we would easily prevail over my father. He would however leave us far behind right out of the gate. It was the only time in life I recall such a competition. It had impressed me that long before we had ever known Dad, he was running through the fields of Kilcoke, his home town, and his school at Knockaroo in County Laois playing hurling with his friends.

As a family we looked forward to special Irish events especially during the summer. My father and mother were so energized by these events and the many friendships that often resulted. One event was an Irish festival of music and dance at Bear Mountain New York. We would all board a large boat in Manhattan and head up the Hudson River to Bear Mountain. The ship would be teeming with Irish families. Interspersed everywhere were musicians playing fiddles, accordions, tin whistles, and banjos, with others skillfully playing spoons on their one hand, and bouncing the spoons off their thighs, as they would mimic Irish step dancing against the Irish reels and jigs that were playing. Perhaps nowhere on planet earth was there to be found such celebration and laughter. It was probably events like these that inspired the song to be written so long ago, *When Irish eyes are smiling*. As children we appreciated our beautiful Irish heritage. The innocence, simplicity and joy of so many people who gathered together celebrating their culture and music. When we disembarked off the boat, we were surrounded by the natural beauty of this scenic place that was dedicated on that particular day for an Irish festival. Thousands of people would attend this festivity. One family that my parents befriended was the Nobles who had one son and a daughter. Their daughter Eileen became best friends with my two oldest sisters. They often visited from the city and would stay for the weekend.

One of the things we enjoyed as a young family were special nights watching 35 mm home movies. My mother at the time filmed everything from birthday parties to communions. As she set up the projector, she would often use her fingers to project different animals on the screen. As children we were amazed at this and often enjoyed it more than watching a family movie.

As a young boy I would often ask my mother for a peddle car. Something about peddle cars mesmerized me from the earliest age. One day it caused pouting and dismay when my father finally brought one home from a job only to realize that I had outgrown my ability to sit in it as my knees were hyperextending out so much that I could not peddle. I was perhaps nine or ten years old. My mother came out and consoled me. Selfishly, I poured out my complaint to a most kind and generous mother who in the course of my entire life never failed toward any request I ever made, even into my adult years. My peddle car was that one and only time. Within a few years of that event, I continued to grow taller. A customer on my paper route was selling a real car for $25. It was one of the early cars boasting power windows and power seats. It was a steal, and I needed my mom to pay for it. She did. It would be impossible to share about all the fun we had after my brother and I converted the old farmland into a perfect figure eight track. My older brother had a British car called a *Hillman* shortly before I got my 1954 Mercury.

Over the course of time as a young teenager, I could handle this car at high speeds racing around the track. I would feel like Mario Andretti racing in the Formula One. Friends from school were always in disbelief that I had my own car, and figure-eight track to accompany it. Over the course of several years, I purchased a number of other cars all the way through high school. Often friends would lay flat on the roof of a car holding on with fingers gripping above the door of the passenger and driver side of the car. As the car approached the bough of an apple tree hanging over the track, the stuntman on top of the car could jump up and grab the branch and be held over the track, and catch the car like Spiderman as it came blasting around the track again. In time with connecting fields and wooded areas with tracks we were able to take the cars considerable distances from our home which was very exciting. In no time, by using borrowed plates, we would go out on the real road, though usually at night.

I remember as a teenager working on one of my track cars and my mom walking towards me. On that particular day something about her face had a transcendent look that I knew would express some piece of good news. Her stride as she walked towards me is etched so favorably upon my memory. "Kieran, I just paid off our mortgage today, we own our house free and clear." My mom had to share this with me. Her dreams had come true. The fortitude of a farmer's daughter from Kerry had prevailed. She lived in the home she loved with all of her heart. Her children were secure and well provided for. The unmovable hurdles of life and hardship, the cruelty of human experience that so often holds up a defiant hand of refusal, had given away to faith and perseverance. It was around that time a new song had come out, "I Never Promised You a Rose Garden." My father never spoke such words to my mother, but her life became metaphorically "a rose garden" of abundance and provision for every need of our family. My mom was a great woman who stood behind a great man. At the time of this writing, it is Mother's Day, 2022, and I miss her sorely with tears.

Although we were now living in Lake Grove, we were still very close to the large lake located one town away called Lake Ronkonkoma. My mother made special effort each year that all of her children would become proficient swimmers. Lake Ronkonkoma conducted classes on every level through the American Red Cross. All of us would learn how to swim at the earliest age, but some of my siblings would advance much further. My sister Marian who would go beyond lifesaving to advanced level and would also receive instructor's certification.

As children we would always hear about the curse that was on Lake Ronkonkoma by an old Indian chief. Every year Lake Ronkonkoma would claim at least two lives. This would happen every year while growing up. As a young boy, I could feel that old Indian chief many a time clasping my leg while swimming. It was an emotion that would often be felt while swimming there.

After becoming a capable swimmer, I always had a desire to be a great diver. I would practice and get so proficient that I could easily stay under and pass far beyond the minute mark. On a particular day, I was down so long that I impressed even myself. When I resurfaced, I could see my mom on the shore pacing hysterically. The hurt I caused her that on that day has remained painfully etched on my mind to this very day. I selfishly repeated that event at eighteen years old on the first date with my wife at the ocean off Long Island. As I became older and could drive myself, Lake Ronkonkoma was not even thought about any longer. Long Island's white sand beaches were incomparable.

One day as a young boy on the way home from church I would sit by the window in our family station wagon and stick my head out the window as I'd watch the airplanes flying at low altitude into the local airport nearby. In a loving gesture my mother beckoned my father to drive to the airport where my father drove up to a small building. My father spoke to a gentleman outside and before I knew it, I was up in the air and flying over Long Island. The pilot allowed me to take the wheel and maneuver the direction of the airplane. It could have been a defining moment in my life as I always wanted to be a pilot, and with other similar opportunities I never followed through. My father showed his love mostly as a giving father. Though not a man who spoke comforting words, he showed his love in living a sacrificial life for his family.

As a young twelve-year-old boy, I got my first paper route. Initially I would do my brother's paper route for around three dollars a week, and give him the proceeds of an additional five dollars. When I got my own route, I was beyond ecstatic. What could I possibly do with around eight dollars a week of my own? It was the first time in life of interfacing with adults not connected to my own family. It was a very enjoyable experience. I loved the daily conversations I had each day with my customers. It also provided opportunity to be away from a noisy house. It was at that time one of the most eventful experiences of my life took place that may have also had a dramatic effect on so many other members of my family, including my mother.

Chapter 18

The Savior's Calling

One day while delivering papers I heard a voice in the very depths of my being that I clearly understood as God speaking to me. It told me that He was going to reveal Himself to me in a way that I did not presently know. My thoughts were that the whole world should know this then, why me? The experience was so disarming it concerned me in that it inferred that something about the present way I was believing was incorrect. Did the Jews have it right? or worse yet, the Muslims? One thing for sure, it could not be the Protestants! This repeated itself over the course of around three days. The final time I had asked God that when it happened to please help me not to shut the door as I knew how deeply rooted in my Catholic faith I was and would not likely to be receptive to anything else.

It would only be a short time later that our next-door neighbor, Beulah Halberstadt would ask my mother if I could go to a youth service with her daughter Donna and nephew David who lived next door to them. He was one of my closest friends. On the particular night that I went, it was the first time that I stepped inside a Protestant church and it would probably have been my last as I did not like the message, or the preaching. On the way home in the car Donna Halberstadt and Dave Furman sat in the front of the car and I sat in the back with a young girl on my left side, who I did not know. The ride home was perhaps less than fifteen minutes, and shortly into the trip she began talking to me about Jesus. My first thought was this was the kind of Protestant that we did not like. As Catholics we also did not like others sharing about their faith to convert us away from the true faith founded by Christ on the apostles. I immediately shut out her words as they were offensive and unsolicited. Then I thought of the words I asked God on my paper route just a couple days before, "Help me not to shut the door on any revelation He would bring of Himself."

As this girl continued to speak on that night her words began to penetrate my heart. She never spoke of any denomination or religion but how God loved us and how He provided a Savior who died for our sins. That without Christ our best works were like a dirty dish rag. That we are saved only by His grace, and that it was to be received by faith only, as His free gift. This girl shone like an angel, and her words penetrated my heart more deeply than anything I had ever heard. I kept asking within myself "God, could it really be that easy?"

We had not even made the final turn onto Hawkins Avenue where I lived, and I was convinced that to be saved I must personally accept Christ into my heart, and that I did not want to miss the free gift of eternal life. It was a one-sided conversation. The girl spoke and I listened, but sitting quietly I said within my own thoughts, "Dear God, this is what you wanted me to hear, please Lord Jesus save me, and come live inside my heart." I said goodbye when the car stopped outside our home. I never saw that girl again. I repeated my prayer before I got into bed and woke up the next morning. I saw everything differently from that point forward. My aunts who were nuns were visiting at that time and brought toys from the orphanage and other things for all of us. At that particular time my aunt gave my mother a Catholic Bible and said, "Give this to Kieran." The timing couldn't have been better. I had new eyes to understand what had been entirely closed beforehand.

Now it would seem everyone I met from a spiritual perspective seemed dead. When I'd go to Mass with my family I'd feel as if I were the only person who was connected to God. My parents seemed to be saying empty prayers. It was also a time where sin became more egregious. As I would go through high school and thereafter, there would be some bad choices with ensuing conviction felt. But prayer was always made for those I love, including myself to be saved on that final day. This experience was never shared with my siblings or parents except many years later when all of us children became adults. I have firmly believed the consistent daily prayers for my family back then resulted in most of my siblings sharing a similar experience. In the gospels we read the words of Jesus, "No man can come to the Father except that the Spirit draw him." When we pray for others, God can through time and circumstance bring them to a saving knowledge of Christ. This happened in a dramatic way to our family. We were all devout Catholics with perhaps two exceptions at the time of this writing. We all needed to receive however a spiritual awakening that was accompanied by a *second birth* that is very essential and required to be saved.

Chapter 19

Our Loving Mother

As a large Irish family, we were very blessed to enjoy the greatest meals every day made by my loving mother. Most meals were meat and potatoes however one of my favorites was American Chop Suey. My mother was the best basic cook I ever knew. She was very poor however at making Italian meals. When my mother made spaghetti the strands of the spaghetti would be stuck together and placed on the dish with sauce that was close to lemonade for thickness. I would wonder how Italians loved their pasta so much. One night as my best friend Harry and I sat at Brunos Italian Restaurant, my friend ordered spaghetti with meatballs. I ordered some other dish. When the meal came out and I saw Harry's dish I couldn't recognize the fantastic meal placed before him. I shared a few bites and was blown away by the taste. "So that's spaghetti! Wow!" When I told my mother she became very upset.

As a young boy shopping at the Bohacks Supermarket in Lake Ronkonkoma my mother would fill to overflowing two large shopping carts. She would then go to the butcher a few doors down called Straub's Market. As a boy when I would accompany her, I always wondered why *Jimmy*, one of the owners, would ask my mom how the previous week's meat was. My mother would invariably have a comment that was often negative. It would sometimes bring an atmosphere of consternation, while there might be upwards of ten people in the store waiting for their order. Years later, I would laugh with my mother as I would share that story with her.

Nearly every week while my mother was food shopping, I would cross the street and visit the stationary store that also sold model airplanes. In a post-World War II era I collected nearly every fighter airplane, bomber, and army tank used in the entire theater of the war. I would stand and excitedly share with my mother why it was so necessary for me to have that particular model. She would listen attentively while standing in the middle of the isle with her wagons and focus entirely on what I was saying. When I was finished speaking she would reach into her pocketbook and hand me two dollar bills. I couldn't wait to go home and build my model. If it was a fighter airplane, it would hang it from the ceiling in my bedroom, depicting perhaps a dogfight with an enemy aircraft.

Throughout life my mother retained that special ability to be insightful towards not only the needs, but the desires of each of her children. My younger siblings showed some athletic skill as young adolescents and my mother had them very involved with sports, especially basketball even becoming their coach. My younger brother Joseph played basketball and was one of the most physically coordinated athletes I ever watched play the game. Years later both Joe and myself played together often and were undefeatable. Two former athletes from our large high school played us on the court one day. It was a battle of the giants. One of the young men was around my age and known as the star athlete of our high school. Because he had the same first name as myself, which was fairly rare, I would jokingly pretend I was him. On that day we took the trophy home which amounted later to farcical bragging rights to my young wife. My brother was the real hero of most of our games, but we were a devastating force together. He would take me aside during critical games and discuss strategy and when and where to place picks and special passes. At seventy during the time of this writing I regularly play basketball with very serious young athletes in their late teens and twenties. My skill level today especially in shooting is far beyond my younger years. Every day on the court is also a time of giving thanks to God for such endowment of physical strength to play young men with boundless energy, dexterity and speed. My earlier years of playing with my brother introduced me to a healthy diversion and passion especially for my later years.

Every birthday and Christmas were unforgettable experiences for all of us children. From the early days of Wiggens Street, my mother made these holidays very special days. As a young boy I recall my mother faithfully placing gifts for each of us under the tree that was precisely what we were expecting. As small children we would wake up to see wine and various breads and snacks that were shared with Santa Clause when he arrived. I had a problem as a very young boy understanding how Santa could fit all of this into his schedule. By the time we lived in Lake Grove there were so many gifts that one could hardly see the tree on Christmas morning. Gifts several feet high would surround the tree far out into the room. I sat one time before Christmas with my mother looking through the Sears catalog and going over different bicycles. There was an expensive chrome bike with a banana seat that had etched flames on the seat with three speed controls and hand brakes. It was the most expensive bike of all the choices. My mother could tell how much I wanted that bike. That Christmas morning it was there under the tree. The excitement of all of us kids running down the stairs early Christmas morning was a memory I will always cherish.

There was never a sparse year growing up. My mother made Christmas the most memorable day of the year, and never neglected to communicate the spiritual significance of why we celebrated this day. Mass was always requisite to all of our Christmases as were all other Holy Days of Obligation. My mother would often define our Irishness as being faithful to attending Mass especially on certain holidays. As all of us became older and began having our own children, we would all converge at my parents' home Christmas night. It was always a spectacular event. My parents now became the recipients of gifts and presents that were lavished upon them. On this day every year their home was the most memorable gathering of our large family. My mother was the matriarch of a large Irish family surrounded by children who loved her, especially daughters who doted on both of my parents, but were undeniably closer to their mother. My father as the patriarch would enjoy these gatherings immensely, aptly engaging conversation and sitting in the place of highest honor in our family with friends and other relatives.

On nearly every family occasion it was customary for my father to give a speech, extemporaneously. He would nearly always share some aspect of their journey together in life along with many references of leaving Ireland and the building of a new life in America. All of this would be a scene my mother as a young girl from Banemore would desire to look into; her home becoming the place where all her children with spouses and grandchildren would celebrate life together. Birthdays also became such special events especially when we were young children. During good weather large tables were placed outside and decorations placed everywhere. Our friends were invited over and we enjoyed a special day that was completely planned for us by my mother.

The joy for young boys of living on what used to be a farm cannot be adequately described. Every day was a new adventure. Large woods and fields were everywhere. A large pond was a favorite place to explore. A nearby old graveyard always frightened me especially when camping out. The epitaphs could still be read from people who lived during the 1700's, who lost their loved ones.

As a young teenager I had the choice of riding my bike to Lake Ronkonkoma and visiting my best friend Harry Swanson or walking behind our home and roaring at high speeds around a figure eight track with one of my cars. In time the enamor of motorcycles and the desire to have one became a daily entreaty to my mother, that would soon be realized at the motorcycle store in a nearby town. My mother would stand there with me as she did for my first car at the age of thirteen. A fair question would be, was I spoiled? In my very depths as a young person, I found within myself a thankfulness to God and a realization of profound sacrifices that were made by both of my parents for all of us children. I would always see God as the great Benefactor of my parents and I was simply a recipient of this blessing and covenant upon their lives.

Chapter 20

Camping

I was still a fairly young teenager when I accompanied my father to a local camper store where my father at my mother's behest bought a camper trailer to be pulled behind the family station wagon. My younger siblings were the primary beneficiaries for many summers of spending weeks at campsites in New York and nearby states. My father would park the trailer at the chosen site and then return back to New York where he himself would continue working.

My infatuation with cars and motorcycles caused me to miss out on several of these family adventures. When I was sixteen, I accompanied our family to Maple Park in Massachusetts. It was so memorable and an awesome place to be as a teenager. A large family in such small quarters and my mother's desire to make such an experience a memorable vacation is something all of us will never forget. I would listen to my sisters tell stories of these campgrounds years later in life and their profound enjoyment of making new friends and the felicity of family being together in the great outdoors.

Gerry and Kieran

Chapter 21

Twitterpated

As this book will invariably be read by my own posterity one day, I have the writer's privilege and also my beloved father's approval to share this story from my own perspective. Although some events may seem ancillary and peripheral, they also define my parents through the lens of others who are not children. When I was seventeen, I decided to ride my motorcycle to visit my friend Lee who was also dating my sister at the time. He was having a party and while visiting I happened to see his aunt who happened to be younger than him. She was only sixteen. She was possibly the prettiest girl I had ever seen. Like my dad years before with my mother I was twitterpated. Unfortunately, I don't think the feelings were mutual at that time as I looked too much like a hood on a motorcycle. After that night I made special effort to visit Lee and find out more about his aunt. Lee would often on these visits touch my motorcycle and poke at things and sit on the front wheel fender as he would speak facing me. One day I made the executive decision that it probably wasn't in the cards for me to meet his beautiful aunt, and I no longer had the grace for his intrusive behavior towards my motorcycle, and away I went.

Within the year we would meet again under more favorable conditions and within three years we were married, while I was still in college. My parents had special affection towards my wife that would transcend the relationship parents most often have with their daughters-in-law. My wife lost her dad just before she turned twenty, and her mom at the age of twenty-seven. My family became her family, and after we were married this remarkable relationship with my wife remained for the many years and decades they were alive.

As our children were younger nearly every Sunday we would stop at my parents and my mother would make an incredible meal for all of us. My children at an early age loved their grandmother and still share their heartfelt memories of being in her home. As my mother became older my wife and her would travel together once a week to the Irish center with my mother's best friend Eileen Reynolds, and take Irish set dancing lessons together. During the summer they would look forward to attending special classes upstate New York on a weekend called a Ceili where they would learn new steps and choreography of Irish set dancing. Set dancing is group dancing performed in ring formation that often includes traditional step dancing. My wife Gerry became a sixth daughter to my mother. My mother often told me how she could confide in my wife about any problem in life and not be concerned about a confidence being divulged to another person or to even myself as her husband.

My wife also fit the exact mold of what my father respected most in people. Her relevance and social propriety caused my father to esteem her. Most of our family enjoyed conversation that was spontaneous and full of energy, perhaps to the point of being superfluous. My father liked my wife's quiet pragmatic style. He had a deep trust for her, and her opinion on various matters, because of her stability and unalterable style and confidentiality.

Kieran with Motorcycle After a Collision

Chapter 22

The 1960's and Early 1970's

The decade of the 1960's was a great era for our young family. My father's drywall business flourished. There was extraordinary population growth on Long Island as major roadways like the Long Island Expressway finally reached exit sixty, Hawkins Avenue where our home was located. This brought volumes of new traffic through Lake Grove past my father's large sign.

The trips by my father to Ireland were becoming more numerous. My mother accompanied my father on occasion. My father, though perhaps unaware, was becoming more engaged in the thing in life that would most define him, the building of a cultural institute that would affect the North American continent for the advancement of Irish culture and music, and provide a suitable platform to run concert tours from Ireland in local chapters across the United States including Canada. These chapters would stretch from Boston to San Francisco.

The many people my father met both in Ireland and North America and his savant ability to remember everything about them enabled him to solicit help and install eminent people who distinguished themselves in leadership ability especially towards the formation of vibrant branches of this cultural institute called Comhaltis Ceoltoiri Eireann.

My mother's willingness and ability to hold down the fort while my father worked two full times jobs and increasingly traveled would be accomplished only by her indomitable spirit and fervent love for her children.

One of the most memorable things about my mother was that she also possessed exceptional physical strength and vitality that made her forever young. When my friends visited from school they were often disarmed by my mother's humor, energy and buoyancy. The very strongest of my friends were weaklings in comparison to feats of strength performed by my mother. We would all have such a laugh when I challenged them that my mother could beat up all of their mothers put together. My attractive feminine wife would not have worked well on the farm my mother grew up on. While we were dating, I would sometimes hold her two hands in my one hand in a macho show of strength. With my mother I had no such ability to be proud of masculine métier.

As a sophomore in high school, I was one of the only students who had a motorcycle. Because it was a lower "cc" motorcycle, I would ride my bike up my road in an opposite direction to swing around and run full throttle till I passed my old bus stop at the fastest possible speed. As I'd pass my friends waiting for the bus, I would raise my four fingers up off my handlebar in a small gesture of salute. It was like, "I used to be one of you guys. but now I am cool, see you at school." One day I was walking on Hawkins Avenue with my friend Dave Furman, and I could hear the screaming RPMs of a motorcycle owned by my boyhood hero Dickie Hallock. He was laying over his tank on a high-performance Ducati motorcycle with straight handlebars passing a whole slew of cars and barely making it in to his own lane before oncoming traffic. I was awestruck by the speed and performance of his bike. My Honda sounded like a lawnmower in comparison. I was resolved to be the proud owner of a Ducati Mach 1. I stopped by one day to see my friend Dick Hallock. He lived on Hawkins Avenue just a short way up the road. He was about five or six years older than me and one of the coolest people who lived in Lake Grove. The next person I needed to speak to was my mother. How can one describe that incomparable attribute of my mother's love, and her open hand throughout all of my life? Decades later her love is still just as fresh in my memory. I became the proud owner of a Ducati Mach 1. I could ride past my old bus stop now at 100 mph if I wanted to, without backing up the road to gain speed. L.O.L.

Years later when I was finished with high school and working full time for my father, I was overpaid by an extraordinarily generous father. I would go to my mother and place monies in her hand as my conscience would hurt to receive more than I deserved. My dad happened to see this transaction one day and was overtly opposed and declarative to both myself and my mother. My parent's generosity towards me was deeply appreciated and not the cause of ever becoming pampered or spoiled. My father's hard labor and sacrifice was always understood by me as a son, especially after I became involved with him in business. My mother's sentience toward all her children has created those salient memories that are treasured for a lifetime.

Having a high-performance bike that was fairly light opened me to a new world of transportation. It also performed incredibly well off-road. My friend Harry Swanson and I were inseparable since I was four years old, and now he was like a fixture on the back of an awesome motorcycle.

It was while I was still the proud owner of a 90 c.c. Honda my friend Dickie Hallock pulled up one morning riding with his young wife on a 750 Royal Enfield. Rather than passing my house, he pulled in to say hello. In the course of conversation, he got off his bike and simply said, "Kieran, take it out, see how it feels." The Royal Enfield at that time was referred to as the Rolls Royce of motorcycles. It was a gesture of trust and confidence not often shared by bikers except in their highest level of friendship and camaraderie. I was just sixteen years old. When I sat on the bike for the first time, I knew what it was like to sit on a magic carpet. A small crack of the throttle felt like a gentle whiplash as the bike became an obedient servant to my every command. I still wanted to buy my Ducati, but already had my sights set on having a large road bike someday. Dickie would take me into Ghost Motorcycles in Port Washington N.Y. to purchase and drive home my new high-performance Ducati that was only made possible through my mother's generosity.

It would not be long however before I was standing in front of the home of Mickey Spagnoli, a popular graduate of Sachem High School five years before my time. He had a pristine 650 BSA Lightning that may have been a notch or two below the Royal Enfield but a very desirable motorcycle to ride. As I engaged the transaction my mother was alongside me. Years later I would hold every argument to my own sons against purchasing a motorcycle to the point that if they insisted, they would have to move out. My dear mother was not so, but permitted that level of risk that allowed me to enjoy an exhilarating life of escapade and adventure. In God's mercy and patience, I survived. Having lost friends and acquaintances, some with horrible injuries, I reflect back with gratitude that my number never came up, and I was spared. It has made me a great believer in angels.

One night when I was eighteen, I had left a shopping center where I had worked delivering prescriptions and was pulled over by a traffic cop only one quarter of a mile up the road. He told me he had me clocked at eighty-six miles per hour in such a short stretch of a single lane road. My back light was out, and that was my only warning by a kind police officer. Nearly every week I would find myself in prayer and meditation that I was playing a game of roulette. I'd often say in my heart, "God, Your hand just spared my life." One day when riding on a wet road, a woman in front of me came to an abrupt stop. Engaging both brakes, my bike went sideways. I was in a slide on a slick road and I could almost feel what would be a crushing blow to my leg as I would hit her bumper at a fairly high speed. In a reflexive action that was both intuitive and instantaneous, I let go of both front and rear brakes that caused my bike to whip back straight and be brought back under control. As I passed her car my knee had barely brushed against her bumper and I was spared what could have been a permanent loss. I have contemplated through life that aspect of intervention that speaks entirely of undeserved mercy and grace. There is not a day in life that I have not reflected upon those multitudinous interventions with gratitude and love to my heavenly Father. These stories could be a book all on their own, that He has not dealt with me according to my sins and failings. It has caused me to develop a quirky embarrassing habit of picking up coins off the ground, even to the one penny. It is my way of telling God that I am thankful for His smallest blessings. I will be thankful always for His mercy and loving kindnesses bestowed to my undeserving life.

Nearly every day I would visit my friend Harry Swanson. One day while driving up to his home through the village of Lake Ronkonkoma, a police officer was driving a three-wheel enclosed vehicle called a Cushman. Somehow our eyes met and I knew he was after something. In my mirror I could see him swing around and turn on his bubble light on top. I quickly turned into a supermarket parking lot and came through the other side and took the back street to Harry's house. As I arrived at his home and walked to the front door, he greeted me and I could tell his concern as he pointed to the Cushman racing towards us. I handed my school books to Harry and got back on my bike and kick started the engine to a roar just as the Cushman was heading up the driveway.

What followed was a chase as the police officer jumped out of his vehicle and pursued me as I blasted through my friends back yard. There was still snow on the ground and my BSA was a far heavier bike than the Ducati. At a quick glance back, the officer had pulled his gun from the holster and commanded me to stop. Evergreen trees had lined the back yard on the right side and I looked for the best opening and barely made it through. I felt like Steve McQueen in The Great Escape. I had no idea why this officer was after me and I was only aware of not having my registration up to date. I rode my bike up the road to an Irish family my parents were friends with called the Deans. I hid my motorcycle in their garage and called my mother. I had told her the whole story and what happened. She came up immediately to bring me home. On the way home I mentioned to her about my books being at my friend Harry Swanson's house. When we arrived there, it was like coming upon a crime scene. When I pulled up to his house, I sheepishly got out of the car with police officers staring me down. The Cushman had been disabled as it had rolled down Harry's driveway during the chase and careened across the street and into the woods. These cops were mad and looking for revenge. I walked nonchalantly from Harry's house back into my mother's car when the one officer said, "That's him!" They quickly pulled over my mother's car and I was half wondering if it was going to be another chase with my mother at the wheel.

As my mother pulled over the officer came around to the passenger side of the vehicle and signaled for me to get out. As he had me out in the street away from the car, he was furious and demanding for me to fess up. I felt completely alone, without the means or disposition to defend myself. I had no expectation of my mother entering the fray. As I was about to cave in and confess, I heard the car door slam and my mother get out of the car. As in a scene from The Quiet Man with Maureen O'Hare and John Wayne, my mother tore into the police officer declaring her son's innocence, and how I was home sick with her all day. The police officer became like a little puppy before my mother's towering, commanding persona.

When it was all ended, I was almost convinced that this was what actually happened. We drove home and I was shaken. My folly and recklessness had brought my mother into my world, as I knew she couldn't help but defend me. I saw a side of my mother that evoked the thought of a bear being robbed of her whelps. For sake of brevity the story did not end. That cop reminded me of Tommy Lee Jones chasing Harrison Ford in The Fugitive. In time I regained confidence and kept to the rules of the road, at least in Lake Ronkonkoma.

My mother had the strongest moral sense of anyone I had ever known. If I did something that harmed someone or stole, I could expect a strong reprimand. I never did those things. I was always able to come clean to my mother and speak honestly to her about everything. One of the last words I said to my mother when she was dying was how much I loved her and that I never once lied to her. As a young boy I would go as far as telling her about the misdeeds of my older brother, which made me a perfect tattler. As I share these stories how much I want to go back and love that person whose life was like a large umbrella stretching over my life during the course of so many years. Whenever I read a passage in the Song of Solomon chapter 8 verse 7, I am reflective of my mother's love and its reach into my life beyond all obstacles and circumstance, "Many waters cannot quench love, neither can the floods drown it."

An October 30, 1986, letter, written by my mother to my brother who at that time was living in the state of Washington, reveals the affection and love towards myself as we were moving as a family to Ireland and selling our home on Long Island. She wrote, "Well if it does happen, I want Jesus to give me strength I never experienced before in my life because this one won't be easy to handle. He is with me 34 years; there isn't a day but he drops by 2 or 3 times. I have become so used to him. Yes Billy, I am sure Kieran and yourself have stolen my heart away…"

Over one month after my mother died, on a cold morning in November, I was up on the north shore of Long Island. I had just signed off on the completion of a large home we had sheetrocked and spackled. As I was leaving, I experienced one of those rare beautiful moments of intonation within my heart. Its cadence was understood as that voice of my heavenly Father to go and visit my mother's grave which was just a few miles up the road in a beautiful wooded area above Long Island Sound. Perhaps it was to be just that moment of quiet reflection of the mother I had loved so dearly. When I had reached the intersection of two roads, I had the competing thought of going to an estimate first. I was sure however that I did not want to compromise this moment. I called and cancelled the appointment. The customer was angry, but I decided to be obedient to the moment in all of its seeming subjectivity. When I arrived at her gravesite, it was so quiet and peaceful. God knew I was still deeply mourning in my heart.

As I was somberly reflecting on her life, I could see on the far end of the graveyard a beautiful butterfly fluttering towards my direction. To see a butterfly on such a cold morning was a surprise. It came directly to my mother's grave and made a full circle and continued on out of sight. It immediately came to my heart that just a short while ago that butterfly existed as one of the most ignoble of all creatures. It went to sleep earthbound within its cocoon, and came out transformed into the most beautiful of all creatures that could fly through the air. I spoke to God in thanksgiving for such a moment of love, condescension, and revelation. The Lord had pulled back the very curtain of death and its profound sting to my life and the vacuum left through my mother's departure. My mother was now in the bliss of heaven as a strong believer in Christ and His redeeming love. Corruption had put on incorruption. She had come out of the cocoon of her earthly body to be clothed with that one which is heavenly. A glorious transformation that awaits all who are in Christ. On that morning, that mystery and truth of our faith and our future union with Christ was visibly displayed to me concerning my mother, which placed within my heart a great cordial of hope. Our faith often will not give place to sight or anything that relies within the reach of our five senses, but I am so glad on that morning I was obedient. A sovereign God can pull back the curtain in ways that will not violate scriptural mandate. "The secret things belong to the Lord our God, but those things which are revealed belong to us and to our children forever." Deuteronomy 29:29

While dating my wife, I went back to high school after coming home for lunch one day. On the way back I could see in the distance a mail truck coming towards me in the opposite lane. He made a quick left turn directly in front of me. I had hardly enough time to apply my brakes and was catapulted into the air as I struck his vehicle. I had a soft landing on someone's lawn and my bike was no longer visible but lay under the truck. It was totaled. Had an angel dispatched just saved my life? I was grateful having escaped death once again.

My very close friend Dave Furman's brother had called me one night who also owned a 650 BSA Lightning. It was a show bike that appeared in Cycle World, a bike magazine. When we would ride together and stop for a hamburger there would always be a small crowd of people that would surround his beautiful bike to gawk. On that particular night Johnny Furman made an offer that was hard to refuse. He was reconfiguring his motorcycle and wanted to give me the custom show parts for free including installation. Could I get the bike over to his garage?

After the bike was finished, I was the proud owner of a bike I never dreamed I could own. My beautiful girlfriend however was no longer willing to risk her life riding with me, nor did she want to lie to her parents anymore who forbade her to ride with me. She was starting to sound like the girl I would marry.

Intuitively I knew she was right and that God had intervened so many times. I was spinning the wheel and the wrong number would eventually turn up. I called Johnny Furman. Could I sell the bike and remunerate him for all the parts and labor? He was fine with me selling the bike and wanted no reimbursement for anything. The bike sold immediately. The era of track cars and motorcycles had officially come to an end. The inviolable love of a mother and a hardworking father who was such a great provider has evoked memories that have lasted a lifetime as it has for all of my siblings and their own respective stories.

Chapter 23

Birth of a Vision-Comhaltas Ceoltoiri Eireann

In early 1951 a group of men dedicated to Irish music in its purest and most traditional form held a meeting together in Dublin on Thomas Street with the purpose of founding an organization that would promote the distinctiveness of Irish culture in all of its venues especially in traditional music, song and dance. My father, when he worked in Dublin as a young man, was good friends with a gentleman whose name was Ned Gorman who was responsible for getting my father a job on the Great Northern Railroad at Amiens Street Dublin. Ned would invite my father to the Pipers Club at 14 Thomas Street in Dublin where he played his pipes as well as the tin whistle. My father enjoyed that privilege of connection to Thomas Street and people like Ned Gorman who were present at the historic meeting of the founding of Comhaltas Ceoltoiri Eireann, Gaelic for *Society of the musicians of Ireland*. My father no doubt would have been part of this group but he had already left to marry my mother in County Kerry, clear on the other side of Ireland. Comhaltas would go on to become the foremost cultural institute of Ireland. Over four hundred branches of this organization C. C. E. would later spring up throughout Ireland and Europe, North America and other parts of the world. My father in his many trips back to Ireland became very familiar with this organization and its charter to promote and foster Irish culture.

At the time of this organization's inception traditional Irish music was experiencing a decline in popularity against contemporary influences. As traditional music became more unappreciated the morale of many great musicians and performers began to also wane. Comhaltas injected a fresh breath of the beauty and distinctiveness of Irish music back to Ireland as something to be embraced as a nation and by Irish people everywhere in the world. The attempt by *sophisticated and trendy* circles in Ireland to antiquate our beautiful culture was unsuccessful largely due to the rapid growth and success of Comhaltas Ceoltoiri Eireann. Irish people everywhere began to fall in love with the Irishness of Ireland as top musicians and artists would perform in the many chapters of C.C.E. throughout the country.

The Irish diaspora throughout the world resulted in far more people of Irish descent living outside Ireland than within. The United States was a primary destination for Irish emigration since the time of the Great Famine. Today nearly ten percent of the population of the United States can trace their roots back to Ireland. There was a great need to facilitate among Irish people in the United States and Canada resources that would enhance their distinct cultural heritage defined in a long established traditional and purest way.

In 1969 my father met a distinguished gentlemen from Ireland, Labhras O'Murchu who had recently led a small group of Irish performers on a U.S. concert tour that were testing the waters for expansion of Comhaltas into North America. In March 1972, my father received a letter from Labhras, National President and Director General of Comhaltis Ceoltoiri Eireann, stating that Comhaltas was anxious to expand into the United States. My father was then recruited to organize a concert tour in several cities to help facilitate this event. Perhaps up to that point everything my father had done was preparing him to take the helm of such an organization and become its North American founder. My father had connections and friendships among Irish people from the state of Maine to San Francisco, California. His many trips to Ireland which amounted to several per year were often involved with participation or attendance of some Irish music or cultural event. Many hundreds of the most talented musicians, performers and culturally intellectual people were known personally by my father.

My father accepted the offer. His involvement in another musical organization IMA, which was waning at the time, provided many new contacts to help build Comhaltas branches around the country with a missionary zeal. In time both Labhras and my father became best friends. The subsequent growth of Comhaltas in North America under my father's directive and his close friendship with Senator Labhras O'Murchu is deserving of a place in the annals of Irish culture and its advancement in the United States and Ireland. As many as 50 branches across the United States and into Canada would eventually form, much of this, accomplished during my father's tenure.

Accepting North American Chairman for Comhaltas Ceoltoiri Eireann, a concert tour from Ireland was immediately planned. Talent from Ireland included notable musicians and *All Ireland* champion performers. The first concert tour was very successful. It was titled "From the Shores of My Native Land." This title taken from a beautiful song sung by Nora Butler, seven times All Ireland singing champion, who was also a member of that first tour in 1972. Every year would carry a new theme. From the Homes of Ireland, was the 1977 title. A Glimpse of the Real Ireland, was the 1981 title. An Irish comedian Paddy Fallon attended many of the tours over the years and performed as a master of Irish comedy to audiences that thoroughly enjoyed his Irish wit and humor.

As chapters of C.C.E. were added throughout the United States and Canada my father became substantially involved with raising money to build a large headquarters building in Dublin, called the Culturlann na h' Eireann that was opened on April 23rd 1976. This beautiful building would facilitate administration and cultural events all during the year. Every year a convention was held there that received delegates from the Provincial Councils of North America, Great Britain, Ireland and other places.

Later on, even more substantial buildings were built throughout Ireland to facilitate the tremendous growth of the organization. Back at home concert tours from Ireland remained the highlight of all events to be looked forward to by the members. Attendance increased each year, and new talent was found to keep each year fresh and invigorating to the audiences. In time, a North American Provincial Convention was held each year in the United States or Canada. My father's leadership helped guide North America to provincial status in 1992, at the first official North American convention in Montreal. He would serve as its first provincial chair until 1996. That convention was held in Toronto, Canada. It was hosted by the members of the Canada Region and the two Toronto branches. This 1996 Convention had some 1000+ members in attendance.

The final concert tour under my father's chairmanship in 1996 was called Irish Celebration and was very successful. All these concerts provided opportunity to showcase and promote Irish culture in the United States and

Canada. These concert tours required very dedicated volunteers and Irish families who provided accommodation to so many of these young performers in their homes. My father's tenure as Chairman for the Province of North America for Comhaltas Ceoltoiri Eireann was 25 years from its inception in 1972 till 1997. He continued thereafter helping the organization as the honorary chairman to grow by working behind the scenes interfacing with the many branches that continued to multiply across America. It would not be until the global pandemic of Covid-19 in 2020 that growth would diminish and concert tours were cancelled.

In the book of Ecclesiastes in the Bible there is a verse properly applied to my father, "Whatever your hand finds to do, do it with all of your might." My father's gift was to organize, to motivate and encourage people in the formation and building of a large Irish cultural organization in the United States and Canada. In a 1996 article in C.C.E. magazine called Treoir an article was written celebrating the 25th anniversary of the growth of the organization in North America. The author of the article used the word *indomitable* in describing my father's energy. I have often used this same word to describe my father in writing about the dynamic energy he possessed in life. At that embryonic stage of C.C.E. in 1972 when it was still experimental and faced a myriad of hurdles he wrote, "Then came Bill McEvoy, that indomitable son of Laois-fiddle player extraordinaire. His leadership and energy demolished all further obstacles and the first Comhaltas Tour of America became a reality in 1972. Bill, now Chairman of the North American Provincial Council of Comhaltas, still coordinates the annual tour." An often-quoted scripture from Proverbs also tells us, "Do not despise the day of small beginnings."

Chapter 24

Comhaltas-a Conduit of Peace and Reconciliation in Northern Ireland

As Comhaltas Ceoltoiri Eireann grew during those early years, the trouble in Northern Ireland between Catholic and Protestant factions was very intense with many fatalities on both sides. My father, as the son of an I.R.A. fighter who spent many years incarcerated by the English, was adamantly opposed to the violence in Northern Ireland. Comhaltas, as a traditional organization for culture and music would become known to be a conduit of peace and reconciliation to the conflict in Northern Ireland. Irish music is enjoyed by people throughout all of Ireland, both North and South. In a profound speech during 2019 at the Comhaltas convention in Dublin, the Director General shared this very thought to the audience. Most Irish people today desire for Ireland to be reunited. The North restored to its rightful place connected to one of the most peaceful, stable and prosperous democracies in the world. It can only happen however in a way that involves peace, negotiation and the predominate will of the people. It is hopeful that the beautiful traditions of Ireland, its culture and music will be contributory to this outcome and also to the mollification of tempers in this long conflict. And I'm sure that prayer by devout people on both sides has been most contributory in the peace Northern Ireland is presently enjoying.

Chapter 25

Special Stories

So much in life that is worth having is accompanied with hardship and sacrifice. Fortitude and perseverance are needed to succeed in life. My father possessed these qualities more than any man I ever knew. Beyond it all, he was passionate about his native country and its distinctive culture. Despite never becoming an accomplished fiddle player, he enjoyed the satisfaction of becoming an All-Ireland winner of Whistling and Lilting competitions. As a young man working with my father, he was fittingly called the whistling spackler. The fast pace of the Irish reels and jigs and the slower plaintive songs and melodies were to be heard everywhere he was working.

There are so many stories of events and experiences with people over the years that it could be a book all by itself if my father were still alive. One particular story I'd like to share is one that I personally experienced while with my father and my son at Lincoln Center in New York City. We went to see a concert of a man who is considered the top Irish fiddler in the world. As my father was at that time in his early nineties and using a walker, we had walked in after everyone else was seated. When the concert began my father quietly took his front row seat. As the acclaimed fiddler finished his first piece, he spoke for a moment to the packed audience of people that "royalty had entered the room," and that he would never be performing on stage if it were not for this man who had just entered, my father. He shared a beautiful story of playing on my father's concert tours where he became recognized. He asked my father to stand and my father stood and turned around and faced the audience in the behemoth room with balconies where the people singularly applauded. It was a great honor to my father.

It was years earlier when traveling to Ireland and visiting with great musicians and traditional purists, my father would often stop in County Clare and visit with this renowned fiddler's father who was also a great fiddler, and well known throughout Ireland. My father would constantly recommend to his friend that his son had a great future as an Irish fiddler. The parents as devout Catholics were concerned about harmful influences on their young son during concert tours and activities that could often accompany Irish galas and parties. My father had solemnly promised if their son would be released and allowed to perform, he would personally watch out for their young talented son. While in New York my father even brought him to our own home in Lake Grove to faithfully keep his promise to his parents. Today, this gentleman is revered as the foremost Irish fiddler in the world, and is an important influence everywhere traditional Irish music is played. He has performed in many of the most well-known concert halls throughout the world.

There would be innumerable people from Ireland that my father also helped get their start in America. As my parents encountered people who became great benefactors to them after arriving in the United States, my father would also reach out to others with the same helping hand. My son as a very successful and talented artist, went into New York City one day to Third Ave. In visiting an Irish pub on this street, he had arrived as a number of musicians were playing Irish music together. It was a perfect opportunity to do a sentimentalized portrait of an Irish pub as the musicians were playing. While asking the bartender for permission, he handed him his card with his name Kevin McEvoy. The bartender asked if he knew a Bill McEvoy, to which my son answered that Bill McEvoy was his grandfather. The bartender shared about my father's continual help in all the hurdles he faced when he first arrived in the United States. The many stories of people who became very acclaimed or those who lived as ordinary, humble, working-class Irish attribute to my father's inflexible love towards his countrymen, and desire to see them succeed.

Gerry and Kieran's Wedding

Chapter 26

The 1970's-a Time of Weddings, Generous Parents and Their Growing Family

The decade of the 1970's was also one of weddings for the oldest three of the nine children. Our Irish family weddings would compete with the Italians or Greeks, and their famous ability to celebrate. Irish music can be very celebratory with polkas, jigs and simple set dancing that involves small circles of people improvising on the floor as they take the lead of a small smattering of experts like my mother, and family friends from Ireland. Music tempos vary between jigs, reels, polkas, my mother would invariably get up for a singular performance, with my father playing the fiddle. My mother's favorite at every wedding was a reel called "The Blackbird." My mother would dance to that piece even at the weddings of some of her grandchildren. The energy and vitality of my mother made her forever seem young. Even when she began to show symptoms of Parkinson's disease in her late seventies my mother remained vibrant for most of the remaining years of her life. As she reached the age of ninety, she would hold the back of a chair and do her Irish step dancing as her children looked on in love. My mother never stopped being the *Dancing Darling* of Kerry till the day she left this world and all those she dearly loved. Although some of our family weddings were more conventional, I don't think any were without the joy and celebration of our Irish heritage.

When I got married in 1973 at the age of 21, I was attending college and working for my father.

My father at that time had a lot on his plate. He was working two full time jobs, and was already very involved with the C.C.E. organization. I was married at the very time of year that he was overseeing a concert tour from Ireland. My future bride had attended a special wedding extravaganza that provided services and products relating to weddings. One of the companies attending provided photography that was far beyond anything we could afford. The owner of the company in realizing this, inquired what kind of occupations or professions we performed. In mentioning drywall services, the gentlemen immediately made an offer that appeared hard to refuse at the time. He owned a home in a very upscale part of Long Island with a large oversized three car garage that needed to be sheetrocked and spackled, ready for paint. At the time my skill level was not high enough to take on such a project, but one request to my father was all that was necessary. He also loved my fiancé from the first time he met her and would do anything for her. On an early Saturday morning we were there at his Cold Spring Harbor home. My father was in high gear and our photography was clinched as a done deal. It was a substantial project by the time it was finished. I began to realize at my early age the craftiness of people. My father put no price on helping us get through one of those expensive hurdles for our wedding.

My wife's brother attended a church with a distinctive building in a nearby town that had a beautiful basement area that we were able to rent for our reception. As we arrived the night before, to our shock and dismay, the church had engaged a large renovation and construction project in the basement without informing us. We stood there in disbelief. I did not know what to do. Would the reception be cancelled? Both of my parents came to evaluate, and my father would again jump into high gear. He went out to one of his local phone company buildings and brought back all kinds of cleaning equipment. My mother secured sheets to cover the entire perimeter of the room where raw studs were exposed. All of us including my beautiful bride spent the entire night working till that following morning of the wedding. The room finally looked presentable and beautiful. Friends stepped in to help with pick-ups and deliveries. The hundred plus guests had no idea what had been accomplished for our fabulous reception.

From the time I was a young boy, I never saw an occasion of my father being cornered or non-plussed. Every problem had a solution. Both of my parents were resilient to every challenge that they faced, but my father entirely without complaint. Before my wife and I left for our honeymoon that evening we sliced open envelops and pulled cash to pay for the band and all the remaining bills. The memory of that time evokes such love and endearment towards two people that are now both gone. My father unlike my mother was not one who easily threw out affirmations like "I love you," but would demonstrate to all of his children love in the most sacrificial and unalloyed sense. When I worked as an accountant, I'd get home late around 6:30 in the evening. I'd have dinner and be off to a side job that I might get to by 7:30 p.m. I'd be so tired even before I started. How ecstatic I'd be on so many occasions my father would have made a special trip out to the job during the day and I could go home and be with my wife and put the children to bed.

As a young spackler in my early twenties, before I worked as an accountant, I did houses for an acclaimed builder who built substantial homes. My father came out often and spent days helping me get through such large projects. At least once a day he would say in an encouraging way, "Now Kieran, if we can just get you on your feet…." My heart would often throb knowing the expenditure of time and effort it cost my father to help me so generously. A large thousand board commercial job in Lake Success, Nassau County would include my father working right alongside me. He would never take any payment.

I don't know in an etymological study of our word for love, if the English language ascribes a definition that explains love in the sacrificial way that both my parents were towards their children. I know in ancient Greek love was translated as eros where we get the word erotic. Love is also translated phileo, where we get the word platonic love as friendship, as a relationship that is marked by the absence of romance or sex. But there was the highest form of love using the word *agape*, which described the kind of love that is sacrificial, where the benefactor considers no cost towards the recipient of that love. Such a word is used in ancient Greek to describe the love of our heavenly Father in sending Christ to suffer and die in payment for our sins. With such agape did our parents love all of their children. These are only a few stories among the innumerable stories of my parents who I sorely miss.

During the seventies and thereafter there began a process of exponential growth within our family as the older children being married began having children. At the time of this writing there are twenty-five grandchildren. The number of great-grandchildren will far exceed grandchildren as there are presently 35 great grandchildren and still counting. My mother's love and connection even to her great grandchildren revealed that part of the human spirit that often seems unfathomable. My parents would regularly visit with us on Sundays as my mother often described our home as her favorite place to be. My son Kevin would visit with his wife and three children where my mother would be so focused on her great grandchildren every Sunday. She would pointedly chide my father for not knowing the names of his great grandchildren. Yet my father would build a bond with my son that would affect his life profoundly. Over the span of many years, they had an indissoluble friendship. My father would visit at my son's art studio and spend hours there with his grandson sharing stories about life.

Chapter 27

Spiritual Renewal in Our Family

As the decade of the 1970's passed at least three of the nine children were married and grandchildren as mentioned began to appear. It was also during that time that something transformational began to happen in our staunch Irish Catholic family. One of my brothers and at least two of my sisters began attending services at a Christian church that was not Roman Catholic. Initially this was known only by my mother who shared her concern with me. As my younger brother was most responsible, I told my mother that I would talk to him and try to assess what was happening.

After speaking with my brother, it was decided that he would meet with my mother and myself at her own home where my brother was still living. On that particular night my older brother had also joined. As we began the discussion, it was very apparent my mother's great concern of any of her children leaving the *Church*. Although initially our discussion was like an inquisition, my conscience began to prevent me from becoming the great defender of the faith in that everything my brother described was the very event I had experienced years earlier, and had prayed nearly every day since that no member of our family would be lost or left behind. God had begun in His faithfulness to answer my prayer to save the members of our family, and now I was standing in opposition to siblings who were experiencing His saving grace. I allowed him to share his heart about his newfound relationship to Christ, and obedience to the gospel. As this very brother had caused my parents, especially my mother, the most grief and consternation, I was relieved that all his beliefs were within acceptable orthodoxy to the Christian faith. He embraced Christ as the Savior of the world and as his very own personal Savior. My mother was composed but

183

shaken. Perhaps myself as a young boy pushing a bicycle on a paper route years before was where all of this started, when the Holy Spirit spoke deep within my heart that He was going to reveal Himself to me. And He did exactly that, and now my younger brother was describing the very same event as also my younger sisters were experiencing one by one.

It may have been the first occasion in our history as an Irish family and of all our ancestry for this to take place. My brother had the courage to share his faith and personal relationship to Christ with other members of our family. I had never done so, even to my wife. Only in prayer would I pray for our family to not be lost but gain heaven on that day.

My mother would confide in me as she often did on things that concerned her. It may have been the most serious matter that our family encountered for many years. In our conversation my mother shared with me the stagnancy she felt as she would repeat rote prayers during Mass. She loved all of her children, and was especially close to her daughters. My heart reached towards my mother and the heartache she was experiencing. As young children we regarded the Roman Catholic faith as our greatest treasure. As a family we never missed Mass, Holy Days of Obligation, or receiving the Sacraments during the year. My mother pointedly shared how the Irish were perhaps the strongest Catholics in the world. We had all attended parochial school despite living in perhaps the best public school district on Long Island at that time. It was a crisis in our family to our parents. Initially my father did not know, and my mother wanted it to stay that way.

When my sister Marian attended a service encouraged by my brother and two other sisters, it became a final straw as to where this thing was going. Marian was the gem of our family. Her effervescent personality and love for people especially my parents sent a shock wave into my mother's heart at the time.

As I felt compelled at my mother's suggestion to visit a service, I found the preaching very disarming, having had my own experience years before. My siblings were becoming followers of Christ, and focused on the knowledge of scripture without traditions. As it was a congregation of mostly young people and a very young pastor, it was also charged with an atmosphere of excitement and energy. My mother was more pleased with my sobriety in trying to evaluate the situation. My mother had always been a woman of true devotion and her closeness to Marian affected her to want to try to understand this phenomenon that was taking place in our family.

Because of the fervor of the church my siblings were attending, I decided on a Sunday morning to visit a gospel church that was local to me, and attend Mass afterward at our local parish. I had lived further out east than the rest of my family. An elderly Norwegian man was the pastor of the church who had been a missionary to Africa twice with his wife. After the service the pastor greeted me at the door and invited me back to the evening service, which I did.

It seemed a much greater comfort to have attended a church that was pastored by a man who was very seasoned in experience and knowledge. At the evening service there was less attendance. At the end of service, the pastor invited people forward for a small time of prayer at the altar and a remarkable event took place. When I was around twenty years old before I was married an oppression had entered my life in just one night that had always seemed inexplicable. It was something I kept to myself and quietly endured. At the end of the prayer at the altar a young woman who was behind me quietly spoke to me that she felt during prayer that I had an oppression on me for a number of years that God was lifting. She said the next morning that I was going to wake up a different man. I went home hardly believing what took place.

The next morning, I woke up entirely different and at peace just as she said. Not one person in the entire church knew me. It was the first experience of many that would take place in our lives and the lives of our children over the years. Satan and his emissaries are something we read about in the gospels, but often we neglect the reality that his wiles continue today and prey upon our lives in ways we could hardly believe or understand. We are not to be ignorant of his devices and schemes to hurt our lives and those we love or miss the gospel's message of salvation. We read in scripture that the devil has come to steal, kill, and destroy. That his primary goal is to prevent the gospel from being understood in its purity, that Christ died for our sins. The apostle Paul in the second book of Corinthians wrote, "If our gospel is hid, it is hid to them that are lost: in whom the god of this world has blinded the minds of them which believe not, lest the glorious light of the gospel of Christ, who is the image of God should shine in unto them."

Having visited this church and liking the pastor, I shared all my feelings with my mother. The pastor wanted to visit our home during the course of a few weeks for a small Bible study. I invited my mother to come out to the first one. As I think back how honored I am at the intimacy and level of trust my mother had towards me. She wanted to understand what was happening, and desired a closeness to God that she yearned for her whole life. On the particular night she came out, she met this elderly pastor who shared with all of us from the Book of Revelation. It was the first time in my mother's life that anyone ministered to her that was not a Roman Catholic priest. At the end of the Bible study my mother had a strong desire to give her life completely and unconditionally to Christ. Her faith was to be implicitly placed in the atoning work of Christ on the cross. She knelt by one of the chairs in our living room and prayed with the pastor. There was never any mention ever made about joining any church or leaving the Catholic Church. My mother received that night that which is promised to every true believer in Christ, the gift of the Holy Spirit. This gift is received only through placing our faith in Christ, and the efficacy of His completed work in His death, burial and resurrection. My mother left our home as a different person. It would have been difficult for my mother in the setting of the church my siblings were attending. The quietness of our home, the closeness of my relationship to my mother, and the gentle spirit of my wife leaves that indelible memory upon my mind of that special night of the person I loved so dearly.

During this time both my mother and I still attended Catholic Church. I would also attend service at the same Bible church. It did not take long before my mother would be attending services at the church my sister Marian had joined. The indissoluble bond between Marian and our mother transcended all of us.

When I would visit our home on Hawkins Avenue in Lake Grove my sisters were so often there with my mother praying over a family crises or other event. My mother became a strong believer and remained the matriarch of her large Irish family.

It was only a matter of time that my father would become aware of the events taking place among his children and ultimately his own wife. My father, putting it mildly, was not pleased. Everything that defined us as an Irish Catholic family had been disrupted. My father as the oldest son of an Irish patriot and I.R.A. fighter was now seeing his children succumbing to what the Irish had resisted through so much of their history. He had always allowed my mother to be the spiritual guide of our family, and now she was carried away with what my father deemed unacceptable. It would take long years until my father became more accepting towards an irrevocable change in our family. My sisters would dote upon my father more than ever, and pray earnestly over his most minor sniffle. He attended special events of his grandchildren in Christian school and related church services. His granddaughter Christine would hold him tightly as a young girl, and beg my father to stop smoking. With tears she prayed for him to quit. It had such an overpowering influence on my father that he did the impossible, and finally stopped smoking, never again to return to cigarettes. Years later my father would attribute his ability to overcome smoking entirely to his granddaughter, and the purity of her love towards him. My mother however still endured his sorrow and disappointment towards her for what had taken place for nearly the remainder of her life. Remarkably my mother had such inviolable strength and fortitude that my father could never gainsay or advance his argument, though ever so vehemently. My mother believed to her death that we are saved only through the grace of God in believing on Christ, and not by any institution whether Protestant or Catholic. The gospel to my mother was the only power of God in saving lost humanity. People needed to embrace Christ as Lord and Savior to be saved.

I always admired my mother's strength of mind and willingness to speak about God's love to all that she would encounter. So many notable people would often visit our home through my father's work in Irish culture and music, and my mother was always ready to share the reason for her hope in Christ to all who might ask. And yet she would do so with propriety and kindness. When Jaqueline Kennedy Onassis was diagnosed with cancer, my mother had written to her the most beautiful thoughtful letter about the Savior's love and the gift of eternal life to all who repent and turn to Him in faith. In my research I found a copy of this letter which conveyed my mother's beautiful experience in Christ, and the joy and peace that filled her life in serving Him. My mother wanted all others rich and poor to abound with the same hope that she experienced.

My mother had a close relative who wounded many people, especially his family, and caused much irreparable damage to innocent lives. On one of her many trips to Ireland it was understood that this particular person was dying. My mother went and visited and spoke to him about forgiveness and God's love. She also left a small book by Billy Graham. She shared with me that as she left the room, she could see him through a glass divider holding the book close to his face as though thoroughly engrossed in it. She could see his lips moving as he intently read the words. This person had lived a grossly evil life. His whole life was as a train wreck. My mother knew the grace of God, and that the vilest offender who truly believed would receive pardon and forgiveness through the cross of Jesus Christ and His atoning work for our sins.

It is hard to imagine that my mother in those early years would suffer so much persecution and rejection from so many relatives and close relationships. Her two sisters as nuns would not attend any of the family weddings in objection to her beliefs, though they were pure and unassailable. Thankfully as years passed relationships were mended. My mother's constancy, steadfastness, and devotion to Christ became accepted to nearly all her important relationships. My mother was the truest friend one could ever find. I personally have never met a person like my mother, who in love for God, and His call on her life, would as the Apostle Paul, after his conversion forsake all for Christ. and all that was esteemed important, especially the approbation of other people.

Chapter 28

The 1980's-a Decade of Weddings

As the 1980's came I had been finished with college for a number of years, but had stayed doing my trade after I graduated. One day I got a call from my best friend Harry Swanson. He was an accounting supervisor at a large corporation on Long Island. There was an opening in the accounting department and he had arranged for me to be interviewed. I took the job and eventually was over a cost accounting system that exceeded 300 million dollars per year. After five years of commuting, the grass began looking greener back in my father's business. Much of the work I did for my father paid far more than I made as an accountant.

In 1985 I left accounting to resume work in the drywall business. It was a good decision. We were able to buy a nicer home at that time in a better area as we now had four children. My father had come over one day and dug a drywell for us. He was in in his early sixties, and I was amazed at his strength and ability to lay block, which was his old trade with Mr. Eilerston when we first arrived in America. I remember he said to me, "Well Kieran, this will be here a long time after I am gone." How I appreciate these memories of my loving father who only knew how to serve his family.

At eighty-four while working on the outside of my sister's house, he fell and damaged his hand. By not getting therapy, it prevented him from properly holding spackling tools. At that time, he had been working every day for customers with smaller jobs. In not ever taking a salary from C.C.E., my father was happy to work as the oldest drywall person on Long Island. He traveled to different parts of the United States, and Ireland at his own expense, attending conventions, meeting people and facilitating the growth of the organization. The many vacations he took with my mother were also paid for by the several jobs he performed each week. This continued until his accidental fall. His savings would thereafter pay for trips to Ireland until his early nineties. When my mom died, my father was nearly ninety-four and shortly after he was able to sell land and continue paying all household expenses, including his 24/7 personal aides. He also provided substantial help to some his children in need.

During the 1980's, six more weddings took place. My youngest sister Kathleen was married in 1989. As I look back on those days of younger siblings getting married it was such a happy time for our family. Weddings provided the greatest joy to my parents, and our entire family as children one by one were married.

It was in 1987 at the age of 64 my father retired from the phone company, having never missed a day in over 30 years. Even with two full time jobs he found time back then to dramatically grow his cultural organization throughout the United States and Canada. When he retired in 1997 as Chairman and Founder, it would consist of more than 33 branches. As my father would often travel to cities throughout the United States and Canada where Irish people lived, there was always a sense of excitement on the installment of new functional branches to the organization. The particular city would be enriched by Irish culture. Parents exposed to the purity and beauty of traditional music and step dance would place their children in lessons that would result in that phenomenon of interest in Irish culture held throughout the United States today. At the time of this writing there are over sixty branches in the United States.

In those early years of developing Comhaltis Ceoltoiri Eireann, my father placed an Irish American step dancer whose name was Michael Flatley on a concert tour. My father personally knew his parents. They were from Chicago. As a prodigy Irish step dancer, Flatley would go on later to create Riverdance that with other shows has played to over 60 million people throughout the world in over 60 countries grossing more than 1 billion dollars. His feet that were calibrated for tap dancing at 35 times per second, held the Guinness Book of World Records and at the time, and were insured for $57.6 million. As my father was a pure traditionalist, I don't think he ever attended one of these popular shows, nor was his fame and early connection to the concert tours ever vaunted. Riverdance with all of its outgrowths would spawn great interest in Irish music and step dancing to people throughout the world. Comhaltis would be the guardian and template of purity and what's truly Irish and traditional. Embellishment for performance can be applauded even by traditional purists like my father, but only within the confines of entertainment. As the coffee commercial from many years ago a special coffee taster would enter a village in South America and taste a cup of coffee from the crop as the anxious villagers looked on hoping for affirmation. An affirmative nod for excellence resulted in great joy, dancing, and celebration in the village, because their product could go to the market, and the village would prosper. Comhaltis Ceoltoiri Eireann, as an umbrella for Irish music and dance would preserve and keep as sacrosanct music that is traditionally defined, while still allowing for those nuances that promote creativity and enjoyment.

Mother and my niece, Mary McEvoy

Chapter 29

Exponential 1990's Growth of an Irish Family

Our family began experiencing exponential growth in the 1990's. Grandchildren were being born left and right till there would eventually be 25, only to be exceeded at this time of writing by the burgeoning number of great grandchildren. An unsurprising quality of my mother was her connectedness to the lives of each of her grandchildren. She would be just as energized on the third round of descendants of great grandchildren. Her failing health would not hinder her inborn capacity to love. When over at my home for dinner she was always completely occupied with her great grandchildren.

Having moved to Tennessee from New York now over two years ago our daughter took the upstairs of our home. In her bathroom is an envelope that contained a flower that my daughter gave my mother 25 years ago. My mother kept the flower in her Bible and returned it in this envelope with such a heartfelt notation: "Colleen, you gave me this beautiful flower about 20 years ago when you were leaving for Bible school, and I kept it in my Bible ever since in memory of you. I love you dearly. Nanny xx." That short note perfectly depicted my mother's loving heart towards all of her grandchildren. The love my mother had for each of her grandchildren was as deep as it was towards her own children. All of the grandchildren were profoundly affected by her life and all those indelible memories that are still held onto.

In 1990 we moved into a new home not far from my parents and other siblings. One of our greatest joys over the years was the regular visits of my parents for dinners on Sundays. During the whole decade of the 1990's we would also have large family gatherings several times every month at my sisters Colleen and Margaret's homes. My brother Joseph and I resumed playing basketball on a regular basis, a sport we shared together many years earlier. Our game together became even more deadly than it was decades earlier. It was in the 1990's that our family became very close to our first cousin Bill Nielson, my mother's older sister's son. We had so many family get-togethers at his lavish home in Northport, Suffolk County. Bill became the closest relative to our family along with Ann Whelan from County Laois Ireland. Bill and Ann are regarded as siblings in our large Irish family. My father's affection to his dear niece in Ireland transcended that of many a father and daughter.

In 1994 my father was greatly honored by his own county in Ireland, County Laois to receive the Man of the Year award. His love for his county in Ireland, and his contribution to advancing Irish culture in the world made him a notable person in Ireland especially among the people of County Laois. It was an extraordinary evening that was televised and attended by dignitaries and people who my father had worked closely with for many years.

In 1995 my mother and I traveled to Israel together. Members of our church with others from the west coast and three pastors and a special guide from Israel accompanied our trip. It was a trip that I will always remember. Our Jewish tour guide was a P.H.D. in archeology and had great reverence towards our beliefs. How remarkable to visit ancient biblical sights that confirmed our faith. My mother stood beside me each and every day. I am grateful for our journey through life together, and the pillar of strength she had always been.

So many years earlier, at my request she quietly brought me forward to a rendition of Bethlehem in the quaint Roman Catholic church that we attended, before the present building was built. As a young boy standing quietly beside my mother, it became a profound memorable spiritual experience. Now we were feeling the same inspiration in the real Bethlehem, my mother still resonating as that tower of faith and spiritual strength. It was perhaps around the mid 1990's that we lost two of our closest relatives, my mother's sisters who were nuns. As they were both retired now and older, they would still visit from their beautiful retreat and retirement home called Hastings on the Hudson in Westchester New York. They were perhaps our closest relatives that we regularly saw since we were very young children. I loved to sit and listen to their conversations with my mother when they visited our home. They never missed a birthday card or graduation event as we were growing up. Only later in life, after they were gone, did I reflect how ardently I missed them and the profound, positive effect they had on the lives of our whole family. My Aunt Sister Mary Bridgetta came to visit my mother by herself and slipped on the tile floor as she walked in the front door. She was taken by ambulance to the local hospital, where it was discovered she had broken her hip. After being transferred back upstate to a hospital near her retreat, she only lived a short while. I was very remorseful that I never saw her or visited her before she had passed. Both she and Sister Richard's passing was like the end of an era to our family that would be irreplaceable.

Years after the passing of my aunts, I received a call from a very distinguished Irish nun who was over an entire order in Bluepoint, Long Island. She had the benefit of living in her own small ranch house next to the convent. Her brother who was wealthy, left money before he died for improvements to her home. It was so therapeutic working for that sweet nun. I shared with her my sorrow at not seeing my Aunt Sr. Mary Brigetta before she died. One day she pointed to a graveyard at the side of the house. She pointed to her very spot where she was to be buried. I had asked if she would graciously tell my aunt in heaven someday how sorry I was not to have been with her before she died. It was a very mollifying moment as we stood there together. I was able to take her to one of my father's Irish concerts. She enjoyed meeting our family. With my aunts gone, I told her we were in desperate need of a surrogate nun. She laughed so heartily.

The 1980's and 1990's in our family was a time when exceptional bonds developed between all the grandchildren of my parents. Our family was so very close at that time. Our children's best friends were their first cousins. My son Kevin and his cousin Jonathan were inseparable, as was my daughter Colleen and her cousin Christine. My son Christian was always with his tomboy cousin Jennifer, and his cousin Mikey. Hardly a week went by without sleepovers.

Laughter and fun were constant amongst such a large group of cousins who became each other's best friend. Now that they are older with their own families many of those relationships continue even among their own children. The family parties especially at my sister Margaret's house were raucous events in the best sense of the word, where high-spirited children were in the midst of every conversation and activity. There was such a serene sense of joy on my parents to see the happiness of such a large healthy family. All of my siblings were very committed parents who loved their children unconditionally. I have observed especially in my sisters over the years, how formidably the baton was passed from my parents and how instinctively it was received by their children to become such loving parents. They would lay their very lives down upon any altar of sacrifice for their children as both of my parents did.

Recently back in New York I visited my sister Margaret and her husband Michael. Her son Ryan has undergone around 27 operations to his colon, some of them major. My sister has brought him each time to the Cleveland Clinic to one of the foremost doctors in the world. Ryan has come close to death many times in his difficult journey with health. On that particular day he walked into the room looking perhaps the healthiest of any person I know. He brought his new baby in who clearly had some of my father's features, especially his ears, which we heartedly laughed about.

Eight months before as they were expecting, Ryan had experienced more medical issues. As I was corresponding with my sister by text at that time, I felt to declare a prayer. "I think Ryan will enter a new phase of life that will bring joy, that will surpass all of his pain. This is my hope and prayer for Ryan. And you Margaret have been right beside him all the way, you will share in the joy of his recovery and restoration. You will hold his baby in your arms as he looks on with joy. All sadness and sorrow will be as waters that pass away, hardly to be remembered, but he will not forget your love and sacrifice." As my sister held his baby in her arms, and Ryan looked across with joy at his mother, I thought of that prayer that was prayed so many months before, and the faithfulness of God to our family.

In Isaiah chapter 44 in verse 26 a beautiful passage, He carries out the words of his servants and fulfills the predictions of His messengers. It would be our greatest desire as God's people to be such, to see all the hard equations in this life, and of those we love to be overruled by that higher law of the Spirit of Life in Christ. We often appeal for this in our most earnest prayers, that the mystery of this subject be revealed, so that the lives of those we love be lifted from despondency, to hope. It is simply called *answered prayer*. As a young father now with a beautiful wife we are believing this to be Ryan's story. He is one of the most resonating and tender young nephews who loves God with all of his heart.

During the decade of the 1990's, my parents made three trips to Hawaii with younger siblings. A trip also to Alaska on a cruise with my younger sister Colleen's husband's parents. They had also traveled to Cancun, Mexico and also Aruba and a cruise to Bermuda. Each time they traveled with some of their children. One of the very enjoyable trips they made was to Eastern Europe on a tour boat that traveled on rivers that would allow stops in each country. It was on that same trip they also visited St. Petersburg in Russia. That trip was enjoyed by my parents alone as were a number of trips they made to Ireland. There would also be numerous camping trips where much of our family would be together with all the grandchildren. One of the favorite places was Schroon Lake in upstate New York. A fairly large Christian organization owned a campground there that my sisters found to be clean and friendly.

My parents would be so joyful as so many members of our family would converge and spend a number of days together. My father always enjoyed a special place of honor with each of his five daughter's husbands. Each of them revered my father on every occasion that we spent together as a family. It would be impossible to communicate the excitement of grandchildren in the midst of camping together in the great outdoors. The special friendships the first cousins had together brought such joy to my siblings as well as my mother and father.

Grand Marshal, County Laois, St. Patrick's Day Parade NYC

Dad with Oldest Great-Grandson

Chapter 30

The New Millennium

As the year 2000 began my father at 77 years old was still going strong with the trade he had conducted for so many years. His strength seemed as if it would never abate. That mantle of blessing invoked by his mother stayed firmly attached to my father his whole life. He could still walk the full length of the St Patrick's Day parade in New York City well into his eighties. When arthritis set in and his knees began to give out, one of his grandsons or one of my sisters would escort him in his wheelchair. He had received the great honor at least once of being chosen as the Grand Marshall representing County Laois, his home county in Ireland, in the New York City parade. His trips to Ireland became even more numerous as Comhaltas Ceoltoiri Eireann was growing substantially on both sides of the Atlantic Ocean. My mother would travel to Ireland with my father at least once a year. It would provide her an opportunity to visit relatives and acquaintances in Kerry and to visit my father's family in County Laois.

On February 21 2000, my parents celebrated their 50th wedding anniversary. It was a very special time of family celebration with everyone attending. If I remember correctly, my parents celebrated this at the Irish American Center in Mineola with a large dance floor and tables for guests and Irish musicians playing. My father, as always, shared a history of their adventure together.

It was probably around 2002 and 2003 that the most difficult events of our family were about to take place. My mother had been fixing her hair at home and had noticed her hand had slight tremors that were not controllable. Around the same time during an Irish set dancing lesson, she had noticed an inability in her leg movements that she had never experienced before. This was very concerning and my mother immediately made an appointment to see a specialist. She was diagnosed with Parkinson's disease, a long-term degenerative disorder of the central nervous system that mainly affects the motor system. The symptoms generally emerge slowly. My mother was 78 years old. I stopped over one morning as she sat with my father at the kitchen table. I placed my hand on her lap and prayed as my mom wept. We strongly believed as a Christian family God's willingness to heal. My mother continued all of her activities, especially Irish step and set dancing for many years to come. As time progressed certain difficult demarcations were reached. My younger brother had to take the car keys from her which was emotionally devastating. My mother was the most proud and independent person I ever knew. She was a fierce fighter. Both she and my wife became even closer at that time as they began taking set dancing lessons together at the Irish American center in Mineola. As two strong women of faith, my mother was greatly consoled by my wife's company.

It was only a short time later that my sister Marian had discovered a lump in her breast that was concerning and went in for a checkup. The results were not favorable. She had stage 3 cancer. She began receiving treatments immediately. I accompanied Marian to one of the early meetings she had with her doctor from Sloan-Kettering. He had said he had seen many patients with Marian's type of cancer survive 13 years. Marian lost her fight with cancer 13 years later in 2016.

Marian was the gem of our family. This family history is dedicated to her. Understandably Marian was shaken with the initial news. It caused a great amount of sorrow to our family. My father beyond all people I knew in life could compartmentalize hard equations and project courage. Marian was perhaps the greatest challenge to that attribute. My mother would find her deepest solace in praying with all of her daughters. There were times early on in Marian's struggle that my mother would look shell shocked as if in trauma. Our family was in its first major crises.

Marian fortunately had many years of remission and my mother's Parkinson's disease was a slow development, and so much of life returned to some level of normalcy. Skiing and snowboarding became an enjoyable recreation to much of our family, especially among the cousins. My own children except my oldest were hooked and became avid snowboarders. My youngest son Christian applied for a policeman's job out west because of his love for skiing. He has lived there over eleven years now as a detective and owns a beautiful home with his wife and children in the Rocky Mountains, where they enjoy the great outdoors and snowboarding during the winter months. Summers in the early 2000's were taken up with jet skis and family gatherings often on a weekly basis. I often borrowed our jet ski and raced across Long Island Sound. Marian lived on a bluff overlooking the Sound, so I would call her on a cell phone and she would come out to wave to me. I would occasionally anchor the jet ski at her private beach and climb the huge flight of stairs to her house and go inside and have a sandwich. This was a novelty we enjoyed together as brother and sister. Marian was a beautiful woman who was vivacious, animated, and full of love.

Marian's dire prognosis gave way to more and more faith and composure from her earlier devastation as she trusted her Savior implicitly. One morning as I headed out to a drywall job on a large home out east, I felt inspired to write a special poem for my sister. I thought of her life as a flower that had wilted initially in her struggle and by the grace of God, she would be soon lifting a new song of spiritual strength and victory.

Marian's Poem:

When sorrows shroud thy life with tears, eclipsing joy of yesteryears.
When wilting flowers' petals fall through midnight battles anguished call.
Then valiant soldiers doth their weapons wield, flaming swords from
sheath with arm in shield.
To go forth in God's mighty strength, to conquer self and foe at length.
As David towards the giant ran, with quickened step he killed the man.
Until at last when thou art seated, with Christ by side, thy foes defeated.
O lilting flower whose petals bloom, again with strength and beauty soon.
Enduring affliction but for a moment, a shining crown by Christ's
atonement.
Noble knight in shining armor, vanquished foe no more to harm her.
Glorious Christ Thy throne resplendent, valiant warrior thy wounds are
mended.

Marian loved my poem and actually became such a warrior in her struggle. Most of her time was caring for the needs of others, especially my parents. I had gone through a difficult struggle medically in 2009 and Marian stood with me and prayed every night. On a particular night I was so sick

201

and I would quote over and over a particular passage from Isaiah chapter 53, "Surely He has born our griefs and carried our sorrows." As I became so sick, I could not repeat the passage, and I would keep saying, "*S*urely, Lord, You said *surely!*" As I lay that night speaking that word, I was healed. I was singing praise as I sank into a velvety sleep. I awoke the next morning with strength and vitality.

A beautiful passage in scripture that when read brings reflection upon the event of that particular night, "In my distress I called upon the Lord, He answered me in the secret place of thunder." I've experienced this provision of mercy throughout much of my life, and have been prompted often to come that throne of grace to obtain mercy and grace to help in that time of need. I could not imagine life without this promise and provision, especially for the healing of all those we love. Marian was the greatest prayer warrior I ever have known. I do not understand the loss of the best person in our family. We see now as through a glass darkly, but on that day, we will see face to face, and will know even as we are known. As I visited Marian nearly every night before she died, she would often say, "Kieran, God's ways are perfect." One night I felt prompted to ask her, Marian, if the only way that Dad could be *saved* was if God took you home, would you consent? My sister looked at me with the most incredulous look I had ever seen on her before and said, "Kieran, of course I would!" Marian was the very warrior of my poem, a valiant knight in shining armor. A flower that wilted, revived and now a flower lilting in song of praise to God in heaven. The very beauty of her God was shining through her.

Beyond the difficulty and tragedy of health issues at that time our family also went through a couple of conflicts that polarized our family. Sadly, as is all too common in so many families, reconciliation was not easily attained. Many years would go by and there would still remain deep divides within our family. The wonderful parties where everyone would be together ended.

This was tragic to my parents especially my mother. The decade of the 2000's and thereafter was a time when many of the grandchildren of my parents were getting married. Weddings were still beautiful and my father still played his fiddle and my mother step danced, but a mark had been left on our gatherings that hopefully time would heal and the grace of God restore. During the first decade of the 2000's the first great grandchild entered the world. My grandson Liam was born to my son Kevin and his wife Margaret. As the first great grandchild of my parents, they were immensely proud. They had lived long enough to see their children's children's children. A demarcation very few reach. With 25 grandchildren, it would only be a matter of time and great grandchildren would outnumber grandchildren. My mother would often say that she felt like Sarah, the wife of Abraham who God had promised their offspring to be as a great multitude.

In 2006 shortly after my oldest son was married, I went with my parents to Ireland with three of my sisters and my niece Christine. It was my father's 117th trip and he was 84 years old and my mother 83. We began our trip on the west side of Ireland and stayed at a home we rented in Killarney for three days. My father referred to my mother's county as the Kingdom of Kerry, as it is often called. Visiting my mother's childhood home and my own birthplace was surreal as we stood together in the same room where I was born and the home where my mother played as a child and grew up. My mother pointed along the fireplace at buttons she painted as a young girl. My mother stood there with us on that day as the last surviving member of a large family. My thoughts resonated at the joys and also the hardships she faced growing up there. The stunning views that could be seen as far out as the blue Atlantic Ocean and the meandering Shannon River as it flowed through a kaleidoscope of every shade of green. From the elevation of Banemore, it is possible to see out to several other counties in the distance. All those great stories of yesteryears that our mother told now seemed to come alive again as we stood together. Her indomitable spirit and faith in God would carry her to a destiny that would surpass her own thoughts and expectations. She would become that matriarch of a large Irish family exceedingly loved by her children. A new world she hoped for awaited her and a life to live there would be realized.

As we traveled from the west side of Ireland including doing the famous Ring of Kerry, we drove south to Cork and then east to rendezvous with my father's family in County Laois.

One of the remarkable endowments of my father as we traveled throughout Ireland was his ability to personalize each place we went with a history or story of that part of the country. Ireland is a country of great musicians and literary giants along with athletes and other notables such as patriots who fought for Irish independence. As we passed a place called Pearson's Bridge in Cork, we might hear about a great piper whose name was Blind Buckley who played his pipes there on Sunday afternoons who is still remembered and where a modern dance hall now exists. And there was be an interesting story to go along with every person mentioned and place we drove through. As we traveled through the many towns and villages, we might hear about a great Kerry footballer, or some notable hurling champion from 75 years ago who lived there. We were constantly intrigued by the many stories. My father had a savant ability even through his nineties to recollect the history of the country he so loved, and the people he emulated as truly Irish and worthy.

As we stopped one day at a beautiful scenic vista and looked out over the wide lush expanse, my father pointed out a beautiful home in the distance nestled in trees, and said, "Could you imagine living there how far from the world's harm you would feel to be?" As he had spoken that and pointed out in the distance, it was the very thought I had conjured even before he said a word.

When we finally arrived in County Laois my father was at his high-water mark to be at the home of his favorite niece Ann Whelan. Her beautiful home in Port Laois had a designated *suite* all for my father and his many trips to Ireland. Both he and my mother were treated beyond royalty with unabashed attention. My father regarded Ann as one of his very own daughters. They had a relationship that spanned decades and only grew closer over time. Ann was also a devoted lover of traditional Irish music and Irish culture. Both she and her husband were teachers and also profoundly and unapologetically Irish. Hardly a week would go by over the many years of their friendship that Ann would miss calling my father. Her husband Eamon a renowned All Ireland footballer, taught history in high school. He was an expert on the subject and also a brilliant conversationalist. We'd often all sit together in their living room listening and discussing about the history of Ireland. I'd often leave their home impressed with the distinctiveness of Ireland as a nation and their love of country and desire for freedom.

Ireland throughout its history fought to disband the tentacles of English domination and oppression to become one of the world's most stable democracies. For many years now England and Ireland have enjoyed a relationship that would hardly have been thought possible by our ancestors. We would visit areas of Laois where my father grew up. One was Kilcoke, Ballybrophy where my father was born on January 19th, 1923. The fields of Knockaroo where he played hurling as a young boy where cars were a rare sight. In a published article my father wrote, "In those early years, we enjoyed our evenings and weekends during the summer, hurling in Dunnes School Garden in Kilcoke, as well as evenings and nights at Murphy's Cross playing pitch and toss and skittles and sometimes just general mischief." He recollected how he would stand on the square in Rathdowney minding the cattle that were for sale. The perhaps hundreds of names of people some living but mostly all dead were all remembered by my father's encyclopedic memory. Shops and stores and supply houses that no longer existed and the people that owned them.

Our visit to Kilcoke where my father grew up was very pleasant. The old homestead is still there. Although now overgrown, the house is still entirely intact but unlivable. A happy home, as my father often described it, surrounded by 27 acres in a Tuscany type area of Ireland with rolling hills and beautiful fields and hedges, not rugged like my mother's County Kerry. His father played the fiddle and his mother the concertina. My father would say that both of his parents were very talented traditional singers, having been raised with it in their respective homes. My father's grandfather on his father's side was considered an accomplished flute player and whistler, while his mother's father and brothers were all fiddle players. My father's mother was a Byrne from the Byrne family of Timahoe, County Laois. They were direct descendants of a notable wandering minstrel Jimmy Byrne the Piper from County Wicklow. My father would in his writings call his home a *Tig an Ceoil*, a house of music. While upstairs in bed at night, my father would hear his parents quietly discussing the daily challenges of life. His mother would pray incessantly about their every need. As a boy he felt responsibility at an early age to do whatever he could to help his parents. He was the oldest of six children.

A visit to Kilcoke would not be complete without also visiting where my father attended church and was baptized and also where he also attended school. There at Knockeroo, my father spoke with such endearment about special boyhood teachers he loved, a Mrs. Campion and Mr. Murray. One time on a particular visit I found it remarkable that he would affectionately point out the grave of Mrs. Campion outside the church at Knockeroo. In traveling around the place where my father grew up, he would point out a spot near the particular road we were driving on that brought back vivid memories from the past. Wide dancing boards were constructed by local carpenters that were placed there. People from around the area came out to watch as musicians would play and the young women would perform their

Irish step dancing. This started in the late 1920's and continued till the 1930's, when the Church frowned on the practice, that the Lord's Day should be observed in a more meaningful way. My father was just a young boy at the time. As it grew in popularity additional boards were placed in surrounding areas throughout County Laois. My father's savant ability would remember places such as Poor Man's Bridge near Durrow, and dancing boards at Crooked Wooden Cross, Ballinaslee Cross and also Killamuck near Abbeyleix. One day as we drove up a narrow road together my father pointed out the very spot where the Kildellig Dancing Board was built. In his writings about this place he would note, "Unlike most other dancing boards this one was not located at a crossroads, but up a very narrow lane that serviced three homes. During the summer months when all things were in bloom, the hawthorn bushes and trees that grew tall on either side of the lane met high above and formed a canopy. It was beneath this canopy of bloom and blossom that it was not unusual to see a shower of swirling blossoms fall softly on the hair of many a beautiful girl as she made her way to the dancing board. The lane also would be covered with fallen bloom which made the scene so beautiful and grand."

Such literary style with its poetic ambience would so describe the character and atmosphere of these special places. It would still bring back vivid heartfelt memories to my father of his early boyhood days. I was surprised when I did a particular google search about these boards that an article by my father came up that was retrieved from the archives of his Comhaltas organization that is headquartered in Dublin, Ireland. The archives of Comhaltas Ceoltoiri Eireann as stated by my father insures "That the native Irish culture and heritage will always be preserved in its richest form." Contributions by my father I'm sure are a recognized resource to all who consult Irish history and culture.

One of the greatest pleasures being around my parents and their Irish friends especially while traveling was listening to the engagement of artful and joyful conversation. Most of the time nothing profound was ever said, but their connectedness to each other was so appealing. Their conversations shared the same values, interests, culture, and often the same stories. Their words and expressions were as resonating to the listener as the sound of an instrument being played masterfully. My father was a masterful conversationalist his whole life till the time he died at nearly 98. As a raconteur of the English language, he hardly spoke about anything that did not have a related story. Years earlier when traveling together we visited his brother Sean in the town of Durrow, County Laois and stopped at the Castle Arms Hotel. Joe Murphy, the owner came out and sat with us for an extended time. I was intrigued by the commonality and connectedness everyone seemed to have with each other that was multiplied over so many people. My mother and her longtime friend Eileen Reynolds would drive to the Irish American center each week. Rarely I would go in with them, but on special occasions when I did, I would be so solaced listening to their conversations about life that perhaps never solved any problems, but revealed friendship and affection in its truest form. My mother stood by her friend until her death many years later.

When my father was in his early nineties, both he and I went together to Ireland. We stayed at my cousin Ann Whelan's as a home base for the week that we were there. On a particular day I brought my father to a special meeting to see his long time and closest friend Senator Labhras O Murchu, Director General of Comhaltas Ceoltoiri Eireann at their beautiful facility in Tipperary. As this was an attractive resort town, and the facility where I dropped my father off was located below a historic castle called Rock of Cashel, I suggested to my father that I would visit the quaint town and castle while he conducted his meeting with his close friend Labhras. After several hours of attractions, I felt it was about time to visit the facility. I had not wanted to intrude on this meeting. When I knocked at the door I was treated like royalty and escorted through the beautiful building to the dining area where my father was sitting by a fire with his distinguished friend. They insisted that I would stay to be served a meal, of which I could hardly refuse the cordiality.

As I sat there within earshot of my father and Labhras in conversation, I was touched by the purity and love these two men had for each other. Their conversation had a profound quality of endearment. They both worked together over a span of many years and built an organization that surpassed perhaps anything they could have expected. But their conversation consisted of mostly enjoyable stories relating to the times they shared together. At the point we were ready to leave, my father in his wheelchair was not facing his friend standing behind him. As I looked up to take control, there was tears in the eyes of his close companion and friend. My father never saw this, but it clearly communicated that their journey was coming to an end and two close friends were sharing a profound moment together. Labhras escorted us to the car with light and uplifting conversation, and stood alone as we pulled away. How I wish I could revisit that day and replay something so eventful and significant to my life.

Perhaps it's an Irish trait but both of my parents were extremely loyal to friends. As a young man working on the large Protestant farm up the road from him, my father met a young woman who was the future mistress of the estate, a Mrs. Pearsey. Her husband in time was to own the entire farm. She befriended my father and would share the cruelty she lived under. She was a very devout Christian woman. My father was as a friend that she could confide in. Years later my father would visit her on nearly every trip to Ireland. In 2006 when my parents, myself, three sisters and a niece visited Ireland together, we stopped in to see her. My father was 83 and she had a few years on him. As we all sat together in her beautiful home. She sat in the middle of all of us engaging the most artful conversation with such wit and propriety. I could not help but admire such loyalty and friendship. Years later when she died at nearly 100, my father lost a very close, longtime friend. Her devout Protestant faith and my father's strong traditional Irish views had never affected their friendship. I know Mrs. Pearsey was dedicated to prayer and she certainly included my father in these invocations of intercession. Perhaps in the mystery of faith, our entire family became the recipients of this devout woman's love.

I loved visiting my father nearly every day before he died. I would love to hear so many fresh new stories. I would also come to bring solace on occasions when close friends as Mrs. Pearcy died. Just listening to the stories that he shared, was a very healthy antidote for sorrow. My father never wallowed in depression or heaviness of heart, but constantly gave tribute to worthy people connected to his life. He would write about the hospitality of the people in my mother's County Kerry where he spent four years after marrying my mother, "Looking back on the day it was one of the most joyous occasions in my life. In addition to being newlyweds, we became associated with the greatest people on earth, friends beyond compare, their likes shall never be again, most have long since passed on. R.I.P." In all my father's correspondence in personal letters to the family and in the cultural world to which he belonged; my father would continually honor those who had recently died. In a letter to our family in 2007, my father wrote concerning friends, "It seems like yesterday that we sent a similar greeting to all. Sadly, we have lost a few since last year, R.I.P., lovely people, kindhearted souls who touched lives in a very special way."

In one of my father's published articles, A Journey Through Life, published in the Comhaltas magazine Treoir, he wrote about one of his trips to Knockarrow parish where many of his boyhood friends are buried. "During my recent trip to Ireland, I visited Knockaroo Cemetery, a place well known to me. It was in that grand old church where I went to Sunday Mass, and made my first communion. Knockeroo is the final resting place for many of my old friends, so many kind and noble souls, wonderful people with whom I laughed, and quaffed through early childhood. As I stood there all alone on a lovely evening in August, shrouded amongst crosses and gravestones, my thoughts went back to coming to school in Knockeroo..."

In a 2008 letter to our family and friends my father wrote, "Twilight falls on a land rich in memories and tradition. The smell of new mown hay in the air. The Corncrake and the Cuckoo echoing in the distance, and the memories of long hot summer days. Fragments of our past are scattered all around us along the roads of Ireland. The old folks are gone, along with their hardships, their pains, but we can never forget them. We honor them in our memory, and think kindly of them for their gentle ways and soft-spoken voices. They also gave us the gift to charm the world with Irish wit. We inherited their music and their culture. the sadness of their songs still lives in our hearts. The headstones and the cemeteries of Ireland pay tribute to those kindly souls who left us a precious legacy of which we can all feel proud."

When traveling in Ireland together with my father, we would always stop and visit with his brother Sean who my father was very close to. Invariably in talking with each other, my father would commend his brother for the upkeep of their parents' grave. In the same 2008 newsletter my father wrote, "As we commemorate the memory of those who have gone to their eternal rewards R.I.P., as the senior member of our family, I want to pay tribute to Sean and thank him for all that he has done to maintain the gravesite of our parents in Durrow cemetery. Not even a weed grows on this hollowed spot, which truly reflects his caring spirit to preserve the memory of two of the greatest people God ever put on the earth. And for that we say thank you Sean.

In 2007 we traveled to Ireland again. My father was 85. It was probably around the 118th trip made to Ireland. During that trip we had the enjoyable time of a large family gathering at my cousin Ann Whelan's home in Portlaoise. All of my father's siblings except his sister Molly, in England were present. Aunt Mollie however attended the family gathering in 2008. As my father later shared, "It was an evening of music and song just like we had in the old days." It was another amazing trip that all of us enjoyed with a different itinerary than the previous year. My father enjoyed sharing about these trips in our family newsletter for friends and family every Christmas.

In 2008 my father having already stepped down since 1997 as the founder and CCE Provincial Chairman for North America began writing his memoirs for the period of March 1972-July 2008. It contained a compilation of letters and documents saved over the years of his involvement with the organization. I believe it was placed in the archives of Ireland as a notable history of an organization and its profound effect in advancing Irish culture. A future book signing would take place in June of 2015 at a Comhaltas event in Parsippany, New Jersey attended by perhaps over one thousand people.

Mom and Dad with an Irish Minister at a Book Signing

Chapter 31

Great Grandchildren, Another Anniversary and Losing Marian

This next decade of 2010 -2020 marks perhaps the most difficult decade for our family in that we would lose my sister Marian and my mother in 2016, and my father in November 2020. But as in the circle of life that God has ordained, great grandchildren would begin their precipitous rise, and both my parents richly enjoyed that rare blessing often not experienced in life of seeing great grandchildren. My sister before her death in 2016 would enjoy two grandchildren being born that she loved to babysit while her daughter worked. Her glamorous daughter Siobhan married in Florence, Italy in 2011. The decade of 2010-2020 had beautiful weddings of grandchildren that were attended by both my parents. My father's trips to Ireland continued until 2019, the year before Covid-19 shut down the world. I enjoyed accompanying my father at least two of his last trips in 2017 and 2019. During our trip to Ireland in 2019, two of my sisters came along. While traveling on the Ring of Kerry, the second day we were driving on the Dingle Peninsula and received a call from a radio personality in Ireland who requested at the end of our day that we would stop at his home outside Tralee so that he might interview my father in his studio. This was a nice segue in that we were going to stay in Tralee that evening. When we arrived at the beautiful home, we were entertained by what my mother would call, the cream of Ireland. As we sat with the gentleman's wife, my father went off to the studio to be interviewed. Years earlier my father was requested to do the same in Dublin over the course of several days. That interview was placed in the archives of Ireland.

During the years 2010 till my mother's death in 2016, my mother came to our home as a ritual on Sundays, my father often accompanying her. My father being a prolific writer and involved in so many phone conversations would sometimes miss. As an avid spectator of Irish football and hurling matches, he often went to the Hibernian center in Islip for special games. But my mother rarely missed her weekly visit and would often refer to our home as being her favorite place to be.

It was in early 2010 on February 21 that my parents celebrated their sixtieth wedding anniversary. After the celebration my father sent out a letter to our family and friends that he called *The road that we traveled together.* In the opening paragraph my father wrote that their marriage was "a gift from God and a privilege accorded to only a few." He would share a comprehensive history of our family since our emigration from Ireland. 2010 was also the last year for us to enjoy our son Christian living with us as he would move out west later that year and be married within the year to his beautiful New York girlfriend. Today he is a senior detective in a large city. They have two beautiful children.

In 2006 my sister Lillian became a registered nurse. Because of financial struggle over the course of many years, my parents were very focused on Lillian and attentive to provide in different ways, especially while she was in school. When she met George and fell in love, they became engaged and got married in 2014. It was one of the rare times that my father wept. He had a deep love for his daughter, who struggled for so many years. More than Lillian meeting her future husband, he was a prince that showed up on the scene. As a devout Christian man his tender spirit has healed the wounds of my sister, and they are perhaps the happiest married couple I know. My mother had prayed for Lillian for many years, and it was the greatest consolation to my parents for Lillian to marry George. As George has recently retired, both he and Lillian have become avid baby-sitters for their grandchildren, and also take vacation trips with their beautiful new motor home.

My mother's last six years were not to any extent sedentary, though for most of these years she would need a full-time aide. My mother had tremors during this time that occurred during different times of the day, making it difficult for her to do the things that she had previously done so easily. During the week, however, she would visit with her daughters and enjoy the new crop of great grandchildren that were now beginning to arrive in small but increasing numbers.

My father during the first part of this decade completed his personal memoirs, and it was published as a book, Memories From a Great and Noble Past. In 2015 at the CCE convention in Parsippany, New Jersey my father conducted his book signing. Many copies were sold. The book was an expository on the history and development Comhaltas Ceoltoiri Eireann in North America under my father's directive. That event had been attended by a large number of people and had included Irish dance competitions called Feis, where many young people were competing. It was held in a very large hotel. As we made our way through the large crowds, my mother who was now in an advanced stage of Parkinson's, and needed assistance with her aide, spoke to her assistant Ava, and instructed her to walk behind. My mother then walked perfectly in comfortable stride as she would stop and greet friends. I was completely taken back by my mother's performance as she appeared entirely to be in good health, and free of tremors. This would define my mother better than anything I know. She was a very proud and dignified person, and would not allow her disease to define her. In about a year's time, plus a little, my mother on her deathbed wore a scarf over her head before her family because of the loss of some hair. Her dignity, beauty and composure stayed to her final breath.

It was during this decade my father also became a member of a group of Irish men called The Bob Morris Band, and he thoroughly enjoyed being one of their fiddlers. When my mother was still alive, they would perform at all family celebrations especially anniversaries and performed also at my sister Lillian and George's wedding. This band regularly played each month until Covid -19 closed down all places of gathering by March of 2020. Each January during the last few years of my father's life we would hold a special birthday celebration in a beautiful catering facility. His Bob Morris Band would play and my father would also participate. He always gave an eloquent and extensive speech to the large group of our family and many friends, and shared the beautiful story of the life that my mother and him shared together. Perhaps the Bob Morris band was my father's greatest pastime in the final years of his life. By doing what he loved to do the most, playing Irish music. After my mother passed, my father would play once a month in Kate's Pub in Smithtown on every third Thursday of the month. Members of our family would show up and order pizza. My father sat in a large circle on the stage with other musicians and played his fiddle. My father was 97 when he last played with this group. There is hardly an example of living a life to its fullest as my father and mother had enjoyed their lives, despite my father's needed wheel chair in his early nineties, and my mother's battle with Parkinson's Disease. She was visiting with my sisters the same day that she entered the hospital, and while there walked around the floors with my wife on one occasion, and with my sisters on other days during her stay in the hospital in her final week.

One of my father's happiest calls to me was to report on my sister's scans as they had been favorable for so many years. As the years transpired after 2010, my sister's markers became concerning. Marian's health was failing. Our family was in crises. The gem of our family was succumbing to cancer.

While fighting for her own health Marian was prescient about the health of our entire family especially my parents. My father was found to have bladder cancer. Marian's advocacy with my sister Lillian who is also a registered nurse saved my father from the cancer spreading. They brought my father in for immediate treatment. By having a cystoscopy performed, the procedure could be accomplished without incision. After successful laser treatment the doctors were satisfied that the cancer had only occurred on the lining of the bladder. Had it gone further it would have spread. Being diligent and proactive Marian suggested my father be brought into Sloan Kettering in New York City for the same procedure. The renowned cancer center was able to locate additional cancer in the same area of his bladder that they were also able to successfully remove. Marian's intuition with my sister Lillian saved my father's life again. Until Marian's health prevented, she would personally accompany my parents on all of their doctor appointments, which were many.

Marian's astuteness as a nurse with high diagnostic abilities would often intimidate doctors, but she would obtain the most advanced treatment for those that she loved. Perhaps thirty years ago she insisted on me going in for a colonoscopy after I shared something concerning to me. What resulted became an argument when Marian insisted on me going to see her personal friend who was the chief gastroenterologist at New York University Hospital in New York City. After refusing, Marian said that if I didn't go, she would never speak to me again. I relented and went. My thoughts upon going there were along the lines, "How does my sister know all these people?" After an endoscopic examination in the office, the doctor communicated that the bleeding I was experiencing was not concerning medically, but the endoscopy had revealed a substantial advanced sessile polyp that even with his experience he was not comfortable trying to remove. He had recommended the foremost gastroenterologist in the world who had a practice on Park Avenue in New York City, a Doctor Jerome Way, who had pioneered the fiber optic technology used everywhere today in colonoscopies. In the mercy of God, the advanced polyp had not yet become cancerous. Marian's forthrightness, despite my objections had saved me from colon cancer. There are too many stories to ever recount of Marian's proactiveness to our entire family. Beyond medical crises she would pray in the most eloquent and sincere way for every situation facing our large family.

It became so difficult for our family as Marian's condition began to significantly deteriorate. My mother was now fighting advanced Parkinson's disease. Marian often visited my parents and lay alongside my father who she loved so much. My father's persona was that he could accomplish anything. He could not however save the daughter he loved so much, who he brought from Ireland as an infant. It was the most difficult chapter in the history of our family.

As the illness progressed to its final stage, Marian was confined to home. Shortly before this, she had accompanied my father for the last time to visit one of his doctors. When he had come out, she was lying over her steering wheel and with tears running down her face, she looked to my father and said "Daddy, I am in awful pain. I wish that God would take me home to Heaven." On her birthday May 31, 2016, several members of our family went to her home. The quiet strength of my mother could not hide her pain and unfathomable love for her daughter. As I looked upon my parents sitting beside their daughter, an inexpressible sorrow was felt that will always be remembered. With all the joys experienced in the life of a family, those intractable sorrows often visit that only the grace of God can heal.

During the couple of months before Marian's death, I would visit almost every night. We prayed together, read and spoke about things. She lay very composed, cognitive and at peace. Perhaps a week before she died her husband said to me one night with such quiet pragmatism that it would not be long for Marian. Jay's voice was somber and disconsolate. As an executive in New York City with a large bank, Jay was a person in our family who most adhered to the unembellished facts. He loved my sister, and provided for Marian and their four children in the most sacrificial way by working long hours and making hard commutes each day for many years. Marian had tremendous love for her Savior. Despite her suffering she would constantly say to me, "Kieran, God's ways are perfect." On the day she died I was asked by my family to break the news to my parents who were at my sister Lillian's house. They had been staying there for a week while my brother Patrick remodeled their master bathroom at their Lake Grove home. When I had entered Lillian's home, both of my parents were sitting in her dining room. They sat motionless at the table. My father made an attempt to speak and only spoke a sentence with quiet resignation. My mother looked straight ahead as if stoic to the news, and then she wept. It was the most painful and sorrowful event in the history of our family. We had hoped for Divine intervention as hitherto so many of our prayers resulted in favorable answers. It was an outcome that was so difficult for all of us to accept. Marian was gone from us. On the day of her funeral, it was so beautiful outside. As I did my devotions that morning, I could not understand how the world could keep going on as if nothing happened. Nature was singing and it seemed so conflicting because of our distress and deep sorrow. Her husband Jay had called me that morning and asked me to be a pallbearer. The pain of the day was so great my father though able to communicate, had no recollection of the day at a later time.

It was within just a short few days after Marian's funeral that my father had seemed to have lost much of his cognitive function. He could not clearly communicate with us at that time, nor we with him. He was 93. After speaking to my mother, we were now in a time of sorrow upon sorrow with such news about my father. I called some special friends of ours who were missionaries. My wife and I financially supported them as they ran a training center in Idaho for young Christian missionaries, who were preparing to go into some very dangerous parts of the world. I begged them to pray for my dad. The following day Andy got back to me and shared how these young people prayed so fervently for my father. Within a short couple of days my father began to regain all of his cognition, and was soon back to being as normal as he was before. I would visit and he was as clear as a bell. How merciful was God, as I could never imagine my father in his great dignity not having his faculties. I called our friends Andy and Kathy and thanked them for their prayers, and for the prayers of their entire team. Jesus said, "Men aught always to pray, and not to faint." My sisters had attributed this to a urinary tract infection, which I had often seen with my father over the years, but never accompanying such mental impairment. Whether through medicine or Divine intervention we were grateful for his health being restored.

With Marian gone from us, our family was permanently changed. My sisters surrounded my parents with unconditional love. They were comforted on every side. For a period of years, I was stopping in nearly every day, and visited no matter how late I got home, and now with Marian gone, I was even more careful to stop by. My parents continued to come to our home for dinner on Sundays, which brought some normalcy as all of us were grieving. At my home my mother would regularly tell me how much she loved me in the course of our conversations. It is one of my most cherished memories of her. She being sick would say nearly every time "Kieran I am going to miss you." My sister Colleen held family events at her large home in Stony Brook to help our entire family to heal, especially Marian's family.

At or around the time of Marian's final struggle with cancer my parents had been paying full time aides 24/7 over a long period of time. Each of my parents needed their own separate aide. With these large expenditures they had also given generously for so many years to many of their children. The depleted finances now became a concern. My father being so trusted by so many of his Irish compatriots was asked to be the executer of a large estate by a wealthy Irish business person. There was no expectation of remuneration when my father accepted this request, but as mandated by the trust a stipend was paid as a fixed amount which became very helpful to my parents at that time. My father provided so well for so long. Now in his nineties a hard reality began to arise. All bills were being paid, but time was running out. That blessing invoked by my grandmother eighty plus years before was still as a scepter placed upon the life of my father. I knew within my heart its immutability and profound efficacy. A real estate developer had inquired about land that my parents owned that for most of its years had been entirely land locked, and now had a street adjoining the property. It was over two acres behind their home. He had offered substantially more than another developer to build three homes, and was willing to pay upfront money immediately to seal the deal. It was far more than my parents needed. My parents now both living with infirmities would never be hampered by financial difficulty again.

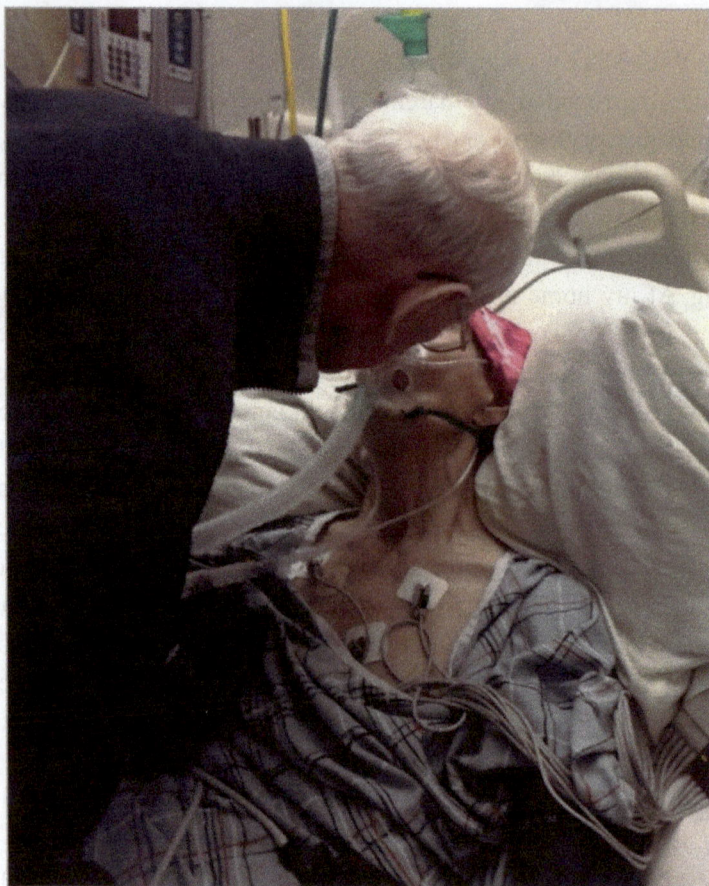

Chapter 32

My Mother's Death

Around the middle of October 2016, I had stopped in to visit my mother. While sitting with her, my sister Colleen came in and after checking her vitals became concerned about my mother's very irregular heartbeat. Her concern caused her to call the ambulance which I had thought was an overreaction. Being as a neanderthal around all of my medical sisters, I kept my peace. As my mother left, I even joked with her, and watched as they placed her on the stretcher. My mother had seemed even cheerful as she left.

Over the course of the next number of days our family visited my mother and she was comfortably walking around the hospital each day. I had every expectation to see my mother coming home at any time. It was not to be. Her condition in just a few days began to rapidly deteriorate. When speaking to my sisters I could hardly believe that my mother was not expected to live. Her battle with Parkinson's disease was coming to an end. Our family was now at vigil in her room. As I approached her bed, I would hear her voice calling me by my endearing pet name, *Keeney*. I am grateful that I was able to speak with her and communicate to her my love. My mother's perfect love was incapable of harsh judgment and I never wanted there to be anything that was untrue to be between us. I communicated to her that I never lied to her on any occasion in my life. There was a closeness I had to my mother that would transcend many of my siblings. Despite her Parkinson's disease my mother had actively engaged life to the very end. Most of those final years she practiced her Irish set dancing with her Irish friends and my wife at the Mineola Irish American Center. She would do this until her late eighties. Several times each week she would visit at the homes of her children. On the night she had been taken to the hospital she had visited with my sister Margaret earlier that day. My mother had breathed her last on that final night of October 21st, 2016. She had looked as an angel on her bed surrounded by those who loved her so much.

Our family again was irrevocably changed. Walking into our home without my mom there was inconceivable to me. The comment was later made by my wife and others in the family that the home had also died. My mother's life had filled our home, and she was no longer there.

My father had shared beautifully at the funeral for over one-half hour the story of their lives together. Only a few months earlier my father was thought to have lost cognition and all rational thought. It was a most extemporaneous, eloquent and beautiful story to all the members and friends of our family. Having my father there brought to all of us the comfort and stability that we all desperately needed. We had only lost Marian a few months before. My best friend Tom Colombo had died only a couple of weeks before my mother. Death had now sent its pale upon our lives in sorrow. At the burial we were only steps away from Marian's grave, where we all somberly stood just a few months before.

How could life ever have normalcy again with Marian gone, and now my mother? I had only in recent days spoken the eulogy at my best friend's funeral. Now our world was forever changed. The many years and decades of visits to my mother's between jobs were now gone. Her attendance to breakfast or lunch, even pouring the milk and stirring my tea would never take place again. My mother always having so much to tell me about what was going on in her world, perhaps being mad at my father about another trip to Ireland, or something going on with one of my siblings. Stories that at the time were so insignificant but now I would give anything to hear again. On every occasion of visit which was almost every day she'd tell me to go into her room and take my 10-minute power nap. I'd come out invigorated and say good-bye to my mother. My children would share the memories of stopping at Nannies for lunch during the week while attending college. My mother was the most beloved grandmother to all of her grandchildren. She had an enlarged capacity to love and an ability to thoughtfully reach into each one of their lives.

When visiting my father each day, I would be expecting my mother to be there as I walked in. The empty feeling of her being gone could not be displaced even by the deep love all of us had for our father. Sixty-six years together was a long time and to wake up one day and to realize a cherished person is gone is a major adjustment and challenge. In an address to our family on the occasion of their 65th wedding anniversary, my father would write, "It is more than just a gathering of family, friends, and loved ones, it is a product of dedicated service to a cause. Raising nine children is a major undertaking by any stretch of the imagination. There were times of great anxiety and concern. It was hard work for both of us as we faced the challenges of life. The fact that we are all here together for this celebration is due entirely to Lily. She played more than a mother's role in the success story of our entire family. Her guiding hand and guiding spirit as a wife and mother are attributes of her greatness."

At the time of this address from my father we hardly knew that in the near future our precious sister and loving mother would no longer be with us. Had it not been for my sisters and so many other people reaching out to my father at that time, his pain and trauma in losing both my sister and my mother would have been unbearable. My sisters would visit constantly and have him stay with them in their homes.

A couple years after my mother died, my sister Kathleen who is married to a successful plastic surgeon, decided to sell her beautiful home in Austin, Texas and move back to New York to be with our family. Her husband had received an offer from a practice in Smithtown, which was local to my parent's home in Lake Grove. It was the greatest consolation to my father that Kathleen would once again be home after living away for several decades. After the move Kathleen decided to forgo working at a local hospital full time and instead would take care of my father and become his full-time caretaker. This decision depicted the endearment of my sisters to my father, and their strategizing for his quality of life, as his ability to walk on his own at that time was entirely gone. Kathleen and her husband stayed at my sister Colleen's substantial home in Stony Brook that had comfortable large upstairs and downstairs quarters. In taking care of my father, she would be giving up an entire salary as a registered nurse and take no remuneration from my father's estate.

Practically every day meant an excursion somewhere, often to one of Long Island's beautiful beaches. Irish events, and his involvement with the Bob Morris Band usually meant a busy week. The full-time aides were kept employed, even though my father was often away with my sister. Kathleen would often take my father to the large Brookhaven senior center where my father would play the fiddle and share his intriguing stories of

Ireland with the senior citizens, most of whom were far younger than himself. He would encourage them to stay far away from despondency. My father would never once embrace any area of negativity or complaint. This would emanate from his person to others, especially those who were hurting and downcast.

After my mother's death one of my father's greatest consolations was communicating with his favorite niece in Ireland, Ann Whelan. Both she my father spoke every week, sometimes more than once. It would bring great solace to my father. Ann was as his very own cherished daughter. She would look up old Irish songs and ballads thought to be lost in antiquity, and play them for my father. My father would relish his last few trips to Ireland and stay in her beautiful home, in her special "honeymoon suite" that had been specially prepared for him. Ann would also travel out after my mother's death to be with my father at his home in Lake Grove. She would visit also with my sisters and my brother Joe, her favorite cousin.

The best part of my day was to stop over and spend time each day with my father. This book would not have been possible without the many stories he shared during that time together. It was especially after my mother died that we developed a closer friendship. He would call me every day and often leave an interesting long message on my voicemail if I didn't pick up.

Chapter 33

2017 Trip to Ireland

My father would travel to Ireland in 2017 and 2019. In 2017 my wife and I accompanied both he and my sister Kathleen.

During that trip my father being 94 had engagements with his Comhaltas organization and members of his family. My sister Kathleen attending to him enabled my wife and I to take excursions together. One day we took a train from Port Laois to Galway. We also drove out to the west side of Ireland to Killarney, County Kerry, a beautiful town to stroll around especially at night. We embarked the next day to do the famous Ring of Kerry, perhaps one of the most scenic areas in all of Ireland. We stayed a night in Tralee and then set out the following morning for the Dingle Peninsula. That same day we stopped by to see my first cousin Buddy in Banmore. While there, we all took a walk over to the house where I was born and where my mother lived as a young girl.

In going back to Port Laois to be with my cousin Ann Whelan, where my sister and my father were staying, we enjoyed the tremendous hospitality of their home. Receiving a call from our close friends Mike and Mary O'Connor in England, they had rented a beautiful time share on the water in County Wicklow and went to meet us there for a couple of days. It was an amazing trip that was enjoyed by everyone. My father's strength revived on this trip as only months before my mom had died. His connection to family and music brought vitality to my father. His beautiful niece treated him as royalty. Their home within the limits of a populated city had many acres of land attached to it. We always felt like celebrities while visiting with Ann. When we returned, my father was a stronger man at 94 years young. He had traveled round trip with first class tickets provided by a generous niece who loved him and cherished having him often at her mansion on the north shore of Long Island.

Years ago, my father and I had a strong disagreement about a business decision that brought conflict into our relationship. It involved his generosity towards an outside party. I had prayed for years that God would enlarge my heart and our relationship would be restored. I didn't think it would be possible, but we became best friends. Our disagreement was as waters that passed away, never again to be mentioned. As long as we live in our frail bodies, we are so prone to sin. Our lives are always in need of God's intervention to bring restoration and redemption.

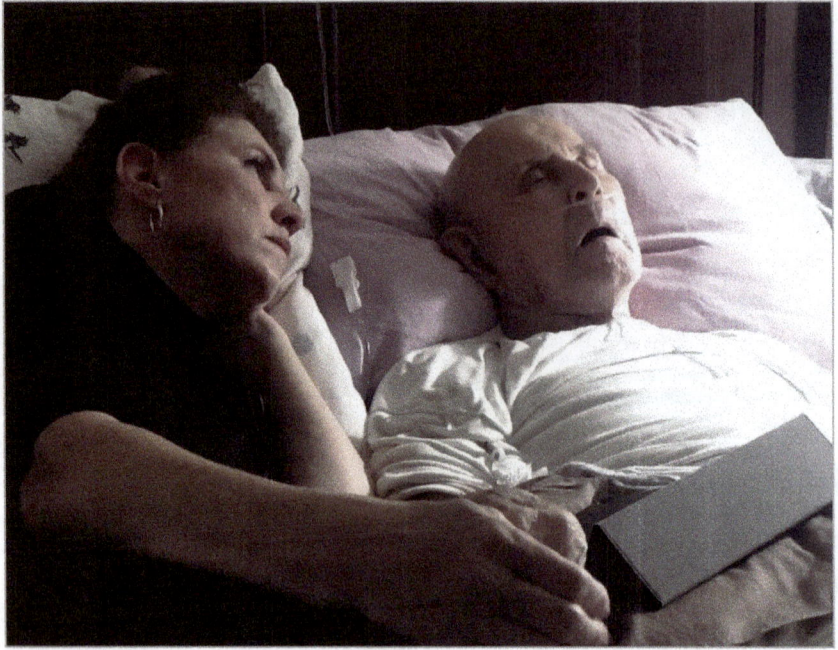

Chapter 34

Life Without Mother, Then Father

When we returned back home it would still be over one year until Kathleen moved to New York from Austin, Texas. In the meantime, my father had his 24/7 aides assisting him. They were kindly Filipinos except for one grouchy guy who really loved my father and was attentive, though somewhat peculiar. My sisters and I visited often, nearly every day. Every so often my father would tell me a story of my mother walking into the room, stopping at the foot of the bed, and then walk straight into the bathroom. My father was always quick to qualify, "Now Kieran, we know that such things don't happen, and I personally do not believe it ever would. And I'm sure it was only a dream." I would always concur with my father. Such a dream would evoke my father's love for my mom and his desire to be with her though she was gone. My father now had a physical infirmity that prevented him from walking, yet his life was full. He was always visiting with his children and grandchildren. My sister Lillian was perhaps the most giving of all his daughters at that time. Her home was his second home away from home.

The 2018 Ireland trip was missed due to a bout with pneumonia. At 95 my father was still young at heart. The mantle of blessing spoken over him by his mother was still overshadowing his life. My sister Kathleen, as the youngest of all the children was held in the highest esteem by my parents and was designated the executer of their estate. She was now there every day with my father. He was doted upon by three daughters all during the week. Kathleen however was there for him exclusively every day as she was not constrained by work. It was her decision that she would forgo working her profession and give her undivided attention to my father's welfare and comfort. The aides remained employed and were allowed to enjoy additional paid personal time when Kathleen would take my father out on their many excursions.

I often called my sister to inquire about their whereabouts and would go meet them at places like West Meadow Beach near Old Field, or at the harbor in Old Stony Brook. Long Island has some of the most scenic beaches to be found on its north and south shores. I would see my father out on one of the boardwalks with my sister as the happiest and most content person one could imagine. This was a common event with my other two sisters when they had my father. There was such joy and affable conversation. The love my father received greatly relieved the loss of his wife and daughter. Likewise, our being with him relieved the loss of our mother and sister. On Sundays he would often be invited up to my sister Margaret's house. Margaret worked significant hours and was not able to see my father as often as my other sisters. She dearly loved my father, and would call him constantly and stop over on the way home from work. For the many years of his involvement with Comhaltis Ceolteoiri Eireann, Margaret being a legal secretary, was his typist. Her husband being a musician from Ireland, would share conversations with my father that the rest of us were unable to engage. He would play the music from DVDs in their home that my father most enjoyed. And every evening I would stop by after work and hear all the details of his adventures during the day. My father's life was so full and overflowing. As I knew by observation and revelation, that my father had an irrevocable mantle of blessing and favor on his life since he was just a boy, there was now a reach by the Holy Spirit to bring my father to that gift and blessing that exceeds all others, the gift of eternal life that can only be received when one embraces Christ as Savior and Lord.

Nearly every time my sister Kathleen took my father out on their excursion, she would play a Billy Graham sermon that my father enjoyed. My father as a strong Roman Catholic would only listen to Billy Graham, as he felt his life was impeccable and free of fault and greed. My father with this exception did not like most Protestant ministers, especially television evangelists.

It would be on my father's death bed that he personally asked Christ into his heart for the forgiveness of sins. At the end of many sermons

232

however, during my sister's outings, my father would reverently bow his head during prayer and invitation. The loss of Marian and my mother was like a plow that cut through my father's heart. Surrounded by the constant love of my sisters I believe he embraced the message of the gospel and free grace of God found only by faith in Christ. He wanted to be in heaven with my mother and his precious daughter who died. Denominational arguments became less after the death of the two people he loved most. His remaining daughters always pointed my father to having a relationship with Jesus as the only way to be saved regardless of one's denomination.

At the end of April 2019, my father was 96, and we went to Ireland again. My sisters Kathleen and Colleen accompanied us. It was to be my father's last trip to Ireland. The following year 2020, Covid-19 would shut down the entire world. This final trip was a remarkable time in Ireland. In Listowel, County Kerry near where I was born, we rented a beautiful room in the Listowel Arms Hotel and invited friends and relatives from the area to meet with us. Refreshments were served and my father was able to share at length the enjoyment of his journey in life and love of Ireland. The endearment of our Irish relatives and friends of our family was so remarkable. It seemed almost ordained that my father's final trip was to be such, surrounded by people who loved him, his countrymen, who knew his love for them was what brought him back 138 times since he had looked out at the fading cliffs of Ireland from the sternpost of the Britannic in 1954 with my mother and three of us children.

While in Listowel we visited a very beautiful cathedral where my sister Marian was baptized. We were able to retrieve that record and then drive to Lixnaw parish to retrieve the baptismal records of my brother Patrick and myself. All baptisms were within just a few days of our birth showing my mother's devotedness to the Roman Catholic faith.

We had another gathering in County Laois at the Killeshan Hotel in Port Laois. My father's many friends and relatives from his own county were there showing the same warmth and affection as only the Irish can do. It was an unforgettable evening. My close friend Mike O'Connor came over from England for this event and stayed with us the remainder of the trip. Mike was the pastor of a thriving church in Manchester, England with his wife Mary. They had been close friends for over thirty years and my father had a special affection for them always asking me about their welfare. Mike and Mary always showed my father and mother a love that has made them uniquely part of our family, as if they were close relatives. My father had respect for Mike and Mary and the sincerity of their lives as true ministers of the gospel. Mike has officiated the weddings for each of my three sons.

Our 2019 trip was planned in such a way that my father could participate in the Comhaltas convention in Belgrave Square, County Dublin and its related events and business meetings. We stayed in a beautiful Royal Marine Hotel overlooking the water in the town of Dun Laoghaire only 7.5 miles south of Dublin City center. On the final night of the convention, it was open to the general public. There was a large turnout. Different step dancers and musicians performed. The master of ceremonies was a well-known speaker and singer in Ireland. As he was sharing with the audience in beautiful Irish oratory, he motioned to my father in the audience as he sang a special Irish song that was dedicated to him. It was so very appropriate as this was the final convention that my father would ever participate in. As profound a moment as this was, it somehow evoked sadness as a final curtain was descending on my father's notable and salient achievements during the course of his entire life.

Not having become acclaimed as a fiddle player, my father realized his true potential by advancing Irish culture everywhere throughout Ireland and the United States including Canada. He helped build the forum for this through the Comhaltas organization with many likeminded people. The talents God gave him were used to create the highest potentiality to do the thing he loved the most, promoting the Irish culture among its own people everywhere. In accomplishing this his life was spent advancing the talents of others who would awaken innumerable Irish to the beauty of their distinctive culture. Young people attracted to this would become future talents that would ensure the Irishness of Ireland and its preservation to future generations.

Leaving Ireland and traveling back to New York was anticlimactic. We had just experienced the most enjoyable trip. My father's buoyancy however was not diminished. His optimistic and cheerful disposition was apparent all the way home from the airport as we all rode together in the limousine. At home my father was once again surrounded by the children he loved. Our mother and Marian's absence would cast a pale over our family that felt like a wound that would not heal. Life would still continue though and provide those moments and cherished memories that will always be kept in our hearts.

Perhaps one of my father's greatest gifts was the ability to compartmentalize and go on with life. While missing my mother and sister, and now in his late nineties, my father was still engaging life to its fullest. World renowned Irish musicians regularly called with the vast array of people he worked with over the many years. He would be invited to sit in at business meetings at the Irish American Center in Mineola or play his fiddle somewhere with the Bob Morris Band, or the Brookhaven senior center in Mt. Sinai. He watched his favorite Irish football and hurling games on his large flatscreen TV in his bedroom. His mind stayed sharp and crystal. As 2019 passed we began hearing about this strange virus in China, little realizing the great impact it was to have on our world. It didn't interfere with his large birthday celebration at the beautiful Windows on the Lake in Lake Ronkonkoma in January 2020. During those early months of 2020, it became more apparent that a worldwide epidemic was happening. My father's world did not change except that there would be no traveling by air. His many other excursions still continued including visits to the homes of all of his daughters. Perhaps in early April 2020, my father and I began talking about the possibility of writing a biography of my mom's story, that would be there for our expanding family. My father wanted his posterity to hear their story as an accurate and true narrative of their lives. It was very appealing and therapeutic for me to receive such a commission. I began writing and became far more attentive to the stories my father would share.

It was during that first week of June 2020, that out of nowhere I developed a sleep issue that as weeks and months transpired it became a real perplexity. Despite running a strong business, I could always sleep well at night without the racing thoughts usually associated with insomnia.

I did not know at the time I was suffering with sleep apnea. My sons thought it was time for me to retire and advised my wife accordingly. Both our second home in Arizona and our main residence in Islandia near my parents' house was put on the market. I know the thought of this hurt my father. Events seemed to transpire very quickly as both homes were very beautiful. This biography commission came to a grinding halt. As I continued to run my business and see my father each day, he showed great concern for my health and gave me advise that was so innocent and pure. He loved me and cared greatly that I was suffering. One day when I stopped by, he spoke words to me that have stuck with me ever since. In the middle of a conversation my father said, "Kieran, I am going to miss you in Tennessee."

We had enjoyed a close relationship for years. I heard stories that made the writing of this book possible. Crippled by arthritis his knees were bone on bone. He would say, "Kieran, I never did the kind of jobs you've done, nor did I get the high prices. I had to get in and get out really quick, so I'd have money to give to your mammy." I would say to my father, "Dad if there was a scale that could measure the work you did, it would nearly weigh as much as the world itself. You took care of your family and gave us wonderful happy lives." I am so grateful that we had such communications as these for years before my father's death.

My father in his later years was able to redefine his relationship with my mother by becoming so attentive to her, and also to so many of his children. He would ask me constantly about one of his estranged children and what could be done, and why did it happen? He also cared deeply about a grandson in Florida that was never heard from. Years earlier he took a special trip there to see him and would often talk to me about it. To the great fault of any member of our family who would ask why I left out detracting stories in this book, it would be the same answer I would give to a noxious critic of President George Washington for having slaves, or General Robert E. Lee for being the Confederate general. Perhaps as a loyal Irishman I might wrongfully disdain Sir Winston Churchill for his polices and persecution of the Irish in his earlier tenure as a Member of Parliament. They were great men who may have been wrong on certain issues or the way they handled things, but history rightly records their contribution, genius and corresponding greatness.

My father was also a great man to our family, his friends and also within the annals of Irish music and culture. He became one of the sweetest and most thoughtful men as he got older. I'd receive a call if there was a special on television about President John Kennedy who we both really liked. If there was a special space launch, etc., I could expect a call. My dad had become my best friend. My mother was the heart of our family that loved us, and sacrificed her life for us in every way. This book could never do justice to the actual lives both parents lived in loving and providing for all of us. In October of 2020, we picked out a home in Tennessee near my oldest son Sean. My wife very much wanted to retire in a place without harsh winters and be near our three grandchildren in Tennessee. Our four grandchildren in New York had grown up seeing us nearly every week since they were born. Our son and his wife in Colorado with two of our grandchildren was not on our list to live near as winters were similar or worse than Long Island.

I came back with regret as decisions were being made too quickly. The relationship with my father was paramount. Also was I ready to retire? Our home contained over thirty years of some of the best memories of our life raising our children. We were scheduled to move the first week of December 2020. My father died only one week before we moved. We moved within a few days of his funeral. It proved to be the most painful event of my life.

On a Tuesday night I went to visit my father at my sister Kathleen's apartment in Stony Brook, at the home of my sister Colleen. I had stopped at the carvel store for ice cream, that my father kept feeding to the dog. We had such a time laughing at my father's mischief. On that Thursday night he became sick. It appeared innocuous at first, just a bug. I stopped by, and became concerned by the weekend that he was very weak. Within a day or two we knew he was dying. He had been listening to Irish music. His lips would move with the light and graceful rhythm of many of the songs he loved. Finally, he did not respond, but quietly fell asleep. It was that Tuesday, November 25, 2020 he breathed his last in the same room he shared with my mom for nearly 62 years. News would quickly spread across the Irish world and among family and friends on both sides of the Atlantic.

I could not be there when they came to remove him, my sisters were so very courageous. The father who lifted me upon his shoulders as a young boy when he surveyed the home and its three acres was now to be carried out lifeless. It was too incongruent and painful for me to bear. It is now over two years since my father's death and the writing of these last paragraphs is accompanied with tears. I hope that future generations may glean from this story the strength and courage of their two ancestors who surmounted and overcame every difficulty and obstacle that stood in their way. That the favor of God should be our chief and primary desire in life, and to obtain at last that heavenly crown that awaits all those who love the Lord Jesus Christ in sincerity. Even now I could only wish that this account of the history of my parents had been first previewed by my father before he died. It is to be placed rather into the hands of all their children, grandchildren and the many generations of posterity yet to follow. I am satisfied that the best effort was made to be accurate with their story without accentuating faults.

In perhaps his final address to our family before my mother's death, my father would write, "Simply put, we did the best we could. Now we say long life to all, and may God bless each and every one of you. Thanks again for the loving care that you bestowed on us always."

  May then every person in our family line live out their lives with the same tenacity, love and fortitude. I pray that all of us and the many close friends of our family embrace that one true faith in our loving Savior who died that none should perish, but that all would be saved. I am so glad that the task is now completed. Any license I took in writing this story and personalizing it was approved by my father. His only concern was that I'd get the job done. And for that I am grateful that it has been finally accomplished. Mom and Dad, I love you both and miss you with all of my heart. Thank you for being such great, caring, loving, giving people. I am so blessed that you were my parents. We will never forget both of you. May all of your children, grandchildren, great grandchildren and those who follow after be inspired! Mom and Dad, Maith sibh! Well Done!

Author Biography

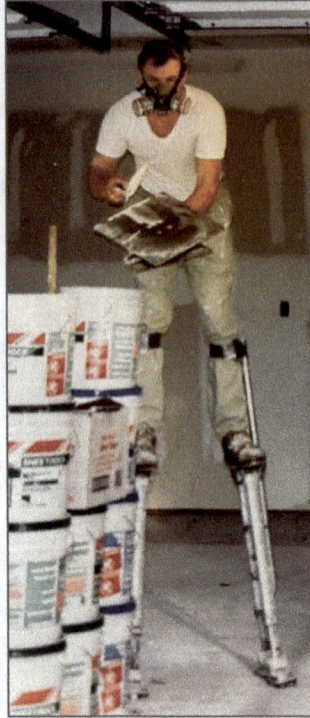

Kieran McEvoy, the second oldest of a large Irish family, worked alongside his father in a family drywall business for over 30 years in Long Island, New York accomplishing over 12,000 jobs. Kieran and his wife Gerry have been married for 50 years. They have four awesome children and nine beautiful grandchildren.

www.ingramcontent.com/pod-product-compliance
Lightning Source LLC
Chambersburg PA
CBHW070119100426
42744CB00010B/1867